IN CONTEMPT OF FATE

The Tale of a Sri Lankan Sold into Servitude,

Who Survived to Tell It

A MEMOIR

BY

Beatrice Fernando

BeaRo Publishing • Merrimac, Massachusetts.

BeaRo Publishing
PO Box 95,
Merrimac, MA 01860
www.bearopublishing.com

First paperback edition, September 2004
Printed in the United States of America

Illustration & Cover Design by
Ryan Feasel

ISBN 0-9759459-0-4

Library of Congress Control Number: 2004094819

DEDICATION

To my mother

Whose love and support I always took for granted. Thank you, Mother, for loving me, even when I was hostile to you. Excuse me for not fulfilling the dream you had for me. Would that I were born again, with all my heart I would chose you to be my mother.

To my son

Who gave me the greatest gift of all – a reason to live. You suffered on account of my mistakes but never complained. Thank you for being who you are and what you have become, a dream realized. You do me proud and I am glad to be the unseen cornerstone of the edifice that you are.

Author's Note

This is my life experience though presented in novel form. Putting it down in black and white meant reliving it – 're-membering' the hurt and the pain, a holistic process however, at the end of which I cried "Father, forgive for they knew not...." So I am the richer for having written it, for now I see the reality of individuals and events differently. My perceptions have been the cause, and they the occasion. So, the publication of my story is but a grateful acknowledgement of their role in my life.

(Names of persons and some places described in this story are fictitious)

Thank you.

ACKNOWLEDGEMENTS

This book would not have been possible without the encouragement and support of my dear husband, Chuty. He made many sacrifices to keep us together and was patient when I stole time from him to work on this story. He believed in my dream and gave me space to make this book a reality.

A number of people were instrumental in bringing my story to the light of day. Linda Kwolek was the first person I shared it with, and it was she who convinced me to go public with it. Sheryl Halvorson, who read the first "draft," an eight-page story, gave me courage to go forward and guided me in the right direction, without any strings attached. Nancy O'Connall edited my first long draft. Jackie Wattenberg, my dearest friend, helped me with my writing and was there for me when I needed her. My heartfelt thanks go out to all these friends.

I am deeply grateful to my editor, Constance Buchanan, who helped me help readers understand the Sri Lankan culture, who generously shared her professional knowledge with me, and who lifted my spirit when I was down. She is a great editor and I am fortunate to have found her.

Last but not least, I appreciate all the support, encouragement, and feedback given to me by the members of the Stoneham Writers group (Andy Gatchell, Bob Wessels, Deborah Nash Angelosanto, Eileen Hugo, Julianne Toomey-Kautz, Paul Angelosanto, Sandy Bernstein, and Sheila Foley) and the Barnes and Noble adult writers group. To all and sundry, many thanks.

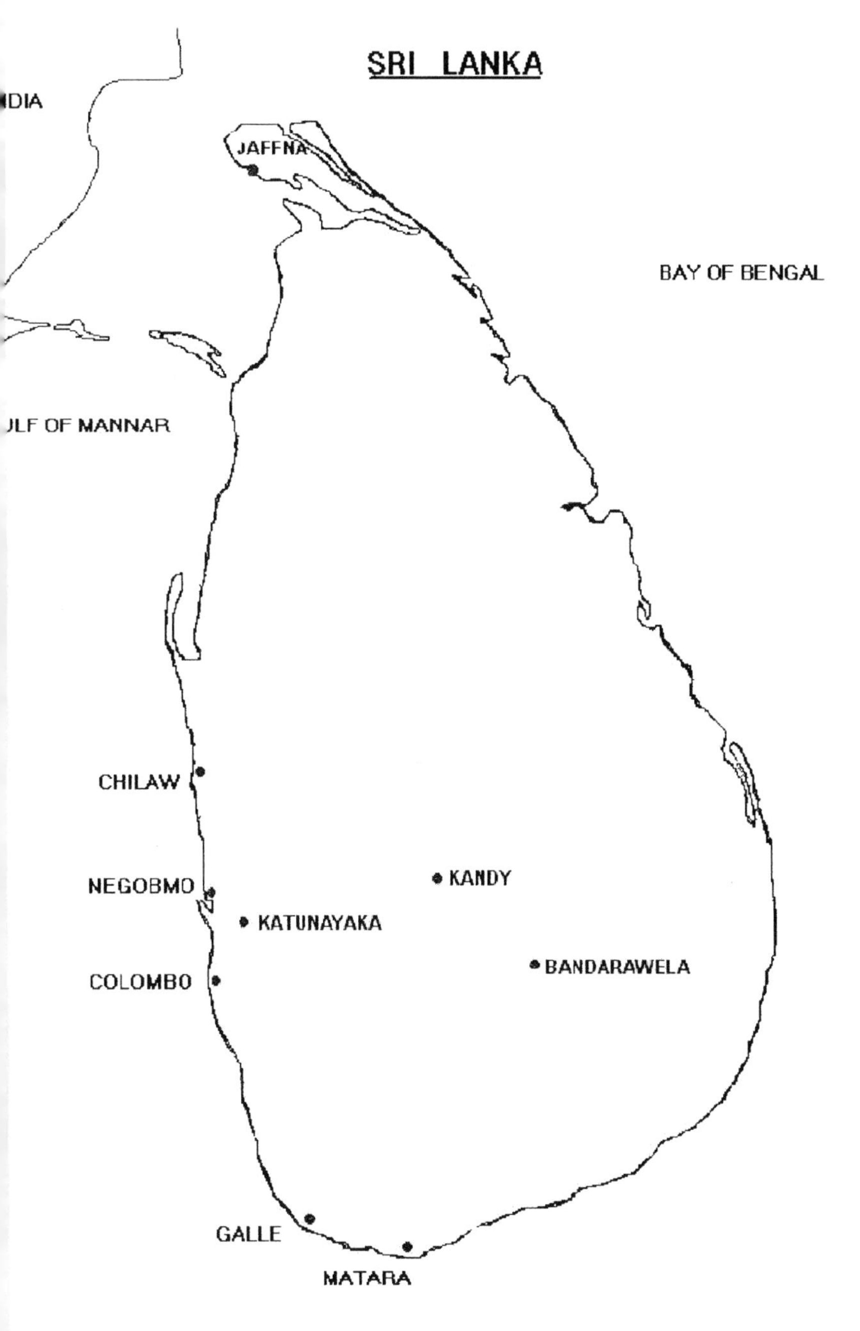
SRI LANKA
DIA
JAFFNA
BAY OF BENGAL
ULF OF MANNAR
CHILAW
NEGOBMO
KATUNAYAKA
KANDY
COLOMBO
BANDARAWELA
GALLE
MATARA
INDIAN OCEAN

IN CONTEMPT OF FATE

PART 1

SOLD INTO SERVITUDE

Chapter 1

About twelve miles from Colombo, the capital of Sri Lanka, that country's only international airport was bustling. People who lived far away had come to the airport early and were camping under the trees, waiting to welcome or say goodbye to loved ones. Only one person was allowed to accompany a passenger inside the terminal. Everyone else had to remain outside in the open, behind a chain-link fence surrounding the runway, while a succession of planes took off and landed.

I sat on a cement bench in the shade of a May tree waiting for Barla, my contact from the employment agency. I had been offered a job as a housemaid for a family in Lebanon, but nothing was certain until Barla handed me my passport and airline ticket. He had kept me waiting for more than an hour.

All around, May tree flowers were falling, carpeting the airport grounds and suffusing the air with their luscious fragrance. The red and yellow petals would dance in the wind, then fall as pitifully and profusely as my recent tears. I needed the job badly, though taking it meant leaving behind Samadha, my three-year-old son. An early afternoon sun beats down, heating up the cement seat. Tickling drops of sweat rolled down my neck and my dress stuck to my sweat-soaked back.

Samadha slept peacefully in my lap, his small mouth slightly open, his breathing shallow and quick. I wiped the perspiration from his forehead and ran my fingers through his damp hair. He moaned and moved. As I leaned over to kiss his face—eyes, cheeks and nose—trying somehow to make up for the two years I'd be away, he opened his eyes. After studying his new surroundings, he wiggled off my lap, ran to the May tree and tried to scale it, shimmying no more than a foot up the trunk before slipping off.

I glanced at my watch. It was getting perilously close to check-in time, and yet the thought of missing the flight filled me with joy. Before leaving home I had given Samadha an audiotape of me singing lullabies and expressing my love for him. I explained that I was going far, far away, to a place where I could make money so that he could have a good life and a good education. But in my heart I wasn't convinced that what was about to happen was in his best interests. It was unnatural, a mother being separated from a young child.

Sitting at a bench several yards away and holding a black umbrella against the sun, my father calmly read his Bible. I had never seen him cry. He was always in control. Not so my mother. Restless, troubled, she leaned against a lamppost and scanned every passing taxi.

"Barla's here!" Amma called suddenly, jabbing with her finger.

I turned toward the bus stop and saw him rushing towards us. "Sorry I'm so late," he said, panting as he handed me my ticket and passport. "You'll be changing flights in Delhi and Bahrain. Mr. Zain will be waiting for you at the Beirut airport. Give him this letter."

My heart breaking, I took my son into my arms and kissed his face, his little hands, his fingers, over and over again.

"Ammy," he said, "when you make a lot of money will you buy me a car?"

Laughing to hide my tears, I hugged him one last time. "I'll buy you anything you want, *putha*. I love you more than anything. If I have money I'll buy you the whole world." Now he played only with empty cans and boxes, whatever he found scrounging around the house. Helpless to provide for his needs, I had no choice in the matter: I had to go to Lebanon. Pappa, a healer and homeopathic doctor who was often without work, could barely make ends meet, and jobs for an unskilled woman like myself were hard to come by in Sri Lanka, especially for a woman who was estranged from her husband.

"Can't I come with you?" Samadha asked, his innocent eyes gazing into mine.

"Ammy is going far away to work for a family," I said soothingly, picking him up. "They won't let me bring you. I'll be too busy working and I won't have any time to spend with you. But I promise to write you every day, and when you miss me you can listen to me sing on the tape. I'll be back before you know it. Until then, you listen to Chamma and Pappa and be a good boy, all right?"

Wrapping his arm around my neck, he rubbed his nose on my shoulder and sighed. I caressed his cheek with mine as I walked over to my mother to kiss her goodbye.

"I'm sorry you have to do this," Amma said, wiping her tears with a handkerchief. "This is not what I had in mind for you, my child, to see you become a servant. It must be your fate. How else could I accept this?"

Fate seemed like a good excuse for my mistakes, but guilt gnawed away at me. Not only was I hurting my mother, I was stealing her dignity as well. My actions were sure to bring shame to the family and start tongues wagging. Sorry is not strong enough to describe how I felt for my mother, who had worked so hard to give her children a good life. Knowing that education was the only way out of the poverty under which we were buried, she had tried her best to see that we had it.

I would have loved nothing more than to go right back home with her, to let her take care of me for another twenty-three years. But that would have been selfish; I refused to be a burden to her any longer. My working in Lebanon was the only way. With that thought, I kissed her again. "Don't be sorry, Amma. You've done more than enough for me, and you still have to take care of Samadha until I return. Please don't worry. I'll be all right as long as I know he's safe with you and Pappa. Don't let his father take him away again. This will only be for two years. When I return I'll have enough money for all of us, and we'll build a nice house. Won't that be nice, Amma?" I smiled to keep tears from spilling down my cheeks.

"I was only five years old when my mother sent me to live with *Achchi*," she went on, refusing to be soothed. "My grandmother made me work like a slave, every day I had to grind one pound of dry hot pepper. When my hands burned like fire, *Achchi* told me to pee on my hands. I remember how awful it was to be a servant. I promised myself then that I would never do that to my children. That's why I didn't let any of you do chores in the house. I wanted you to enjoy being children, at least under my roof. But today, I'm letting you go to work as a servant in some faraway household, with unknown people. How can I bear this pain?"

"You're not sending me anywhere, *Amma*. This is my choice, what I have to do for my child. I can handle this. Don't worry about me, I'll come back in one piece." I kissed her face and walked away.

"Take care of yourself," my father said, scooping Samadha into his arms. "Write to us as soon as you're settled."

After kissing my son's pouting face one last time, I hurried into the airport without looking back. My chest tightened and I felt sick to my stomach. Despite the rush I struggled to put one foot in front of the other.

I was a robot going through the motions at customs and immigration. Then I found myself sitting in the plane, peering through the window and frantically searching for Samadha's face among the crowd behind the fence.

The aircraft was full. The hostesses had their heads covered with silk shawls and they wore green Salvar Camis—loose pants with long-sleeved dresses slit below the hips. I heard bits and pieces of the emergency procedure demonstration as the plane started to move. It felt as if the wheels were crushing my heart. Where was he? I wondered, craning my neck as the plane took off. The people, roads and buildings became miniaturized versions of themselves, then the island of Sri Lanka itself grew smaller and smaller, until all I could see was a green teardrop in a gray sea.

When the plane cleared the clouds I looked down and my head started to spin. I rose unsteadily to my feet, praying that I would make it to the bathroom. The gentleman next to me handed over a brown bag. "If you feel sick, use this," he said. "Don't try to walk now or it'll get worse. Bend over and put your head between your knees."

After filling two bags, I felt better. "Thank you," I muttered. "This is new to me."

Without a comment, he rose from his seat and walked over to an old woman who was struggling with her luggage, trying to place it in the storage compartment. "Here, let me help you, madam," he said.

"God bless you, son, thank you," she said and handed him the bag. The compartment was already full, but he moved things around and made room for the old woman's luggage, then came back to his seat.

He was a dark-skinned, middle-aged man in a coat and tie, about five feet tall, with black hair combed sideways. His polished shoes showed no sign of dust. Out of the corner of my eye, I could see him watching me. I didn't feel like talking, but I couldn't very well ignore him.

"You look sad," he said.

Unsettled by his remark, I stared at him suspiciously. Why should a stranger care?

"Sorry, I didn't mean to embarrass you," he said.

I looked back out the window. Below, mountains of thick white clouds filled a brilliant blue sky, and there was no sign of earth. My son was down there somewhere, far, far away. Was he still crying? My arms ached to hold him. *Ammy!* His sweet voice echoed in my head.

How painful it must be for a parent to lose a child, I thought. The worst pain a human being could possibly suffer. But I hadn't lost him. If I were lucky enough to get a nice family and a good salary, in two short years I would return, and I would never, ever leave him again.

Still dizzy, now I had a headache to boot. I pushed the button for a hostess and requested some Panadole, a pain medicine. The gentleman next to me said, "You don't have to be afraid of me—my name is Bandula," and handed me his card. It read *Bandula Athukorala, Executive Director*, and listed an address in Colombo, Sri Lanka.

"My name's Ranga," I said, relieved. "I'm glad you're a Sri Lankan."

He smiled. His teeth looked bright white next to his dark brown lips. "Where are you going?"

Leaving Sri Lanka to become a maid in Lebanon, I thought, too ashamed to admit it. But I didn't feel like lying, and so after a moment's hesitation told him the truth.

"Why are you going to Lebanon? Can't you find a job in Sri Lanka?" He glanced at my wedding ring. "Where's your husband?"

"You ask a lot of questions," I answered, rather defensively. "I have my reasons for making this choice."

"I have no right to ask you all these questions, of course, but if I could prevent you from getting hurt, I'd like to try."

"This is the only way for me to make money quickly," I stammered. "How can I get hurt doing that?"

He looked straight at me. "Don't you read the papers? Haven't you read about what has happened to girls who go to Lebanon to work as maids? They're abused and raped, and some are even killed. Is it worth the money to risk having any of those things happening to you?"

Indeed, the papers had run stories about incidents like these, and I had read them, but I hadn't given them serious consideration. "Are these stories really . . . true?"

"Yes, they are!" he said, and lowering his voice added, "Don't go to Lebanon. When you arrive in Delhi, turn around and go back home. I'm going to London now, but I'll be back in Colombo in about three months. I'll help you find a job in Sri Lanka. I can promise you that."

Had I heard him right? Could I really go home to my son and have a job in three months? But why should I trust this man? *Amma's* warning echoed in my head: *Don't ever accept help from a man. You will end up paying him with your soul.* I had only known this passenger for an hour—why would he want to help me, a stranger? Bandula looked kind and concerned, but all I could think about was the hard-earned money my parents had paid to the agency and all the heartache I had caused them over the years.

Catholics turned Seventh Day Adventists, they had brought me up with strict discipline. My free spirit had rebelled against the rules of the Seventh Day Adventists and the tight strictures of Sri Lankan society. In church as a teenager, I had committed the sin of passing love notes hidden inside a hymnal to a fellow Adventist, a boy close to my age. Though the two of us had barely ever spoken, we were smitten with one another, and when our clandestine love was found out tongues began wagging. My transgression brought shame upon the family, and Pappa administered a harsh whipping to get me back in line.

His remedy didn't work. Years later I was still a rebel. It was the custom in Sri Lanka for marriages to be arranged by parents after children had completed their education. Anxious to leave home, and ignoring my parents' efforts to steer me toward higher education, I eloped with a man I hardly knew. Tilak was a Buddhist from a nearby village who worked for a company that assembled radios.

Soon enough I became pregnant. It was also the custom in Sri Lanka for a mother to care for a pregnant daughter or daughter-in-law until and after the baby is born. No sooner had the doctor confirmed my condition than I left the apartment Tilak and I were renting and went running back to my mother, who accepted me with open arms. Within a few months Tilak lost his job and went to live with his own mother. Samadha and I moved in with my mother-in-law, but as time went on and Tilak became more financially dependent on her, we grew apart and I returned to my parents' house with my son.

My parents, for all their strictness in raising me, were generous now that I was a mother, but they paid a price for their generosity. Sri Lankan couples were expected to stay married under any circumstances—the divorce rate was only one in a thousand. Technically I wasn't divorced, but in moving back to my parents' house without Tilak, I brought further shame upon the family. Society branded me, and by implication, my parents.

Despite all the grief my ill-considered elopement had caused, I ended up with a special gift—Samadha. My single goal in life became giving him a better life. And if giving him a better life meant being a housemaid for strangers in Lebanon, so be it.

Outside, the plane began its descent into Delhi. I thought again about the hard-earned money my parents had paid to the agency. If I followed Bandula's advice and returned to Sri Lanka, who would pay it back? Even if this man sitting next to me could be trusted, I didn't have enough money to buy a return ticket. Nothing terrible will happen to me, I tried to reassure myself. I'll be careful. I repeated the words over and over again.

Chapter 2

By the time the plane out of Delhi landed in Beirut, my fear of an uncertain future had overtaken the sadness about leaving Samadha. My hands were shaking and my knees felt weak. Bandula's words echoed in my head: *Haven't you read about what has happened to girls who go to Lebanon to work as maids?*

As I walked toward the terminal, a few yards away on the runway, a plane took off with a deafening roar. With an empty feeling, I looked up to see it fly away. Maybe it was flying to Sri Lanka, I thought.

I followed the other passengers through a long corridor that led toward the immigration-processing area. Three counters were open and I stood at the end of the longest line to wait my turn, studying my surroundings, seeing things as if through a screen door.

The line moved quickly. The officer behind the counter, a sleepy-looking fellow with a frown, wore a white uniform and a white hat with black trim. I smiled and handed him my passport. His lips moved as if in response to my smile, but the expression on his face remained the same. Then his big hand came slamming down with the stamp, leaving a seal on my passport. That was all. I was free to enter Lebanon. Collecting my luggage, I went through customs and followed signs to the waiting area.

Barla had said that a gentleman from the agency was going to meet me at the airport, but how was I going to recognize him? What if he were not there to pick me up? Overcome by fear, I decided to wait inside the terminal and ask a police officer for help.

When I went through the swinging door to the waiting area and waded into the crowd, however, I spied a gentlemen at the gate holding a sign with my name on it. Thank God, I wasn't going to be stranded.

A tall, skinny man who looked to be in his early forties approached me with a smile plastered on his face.

"Miss Suriya?"

"Yes, that's me. You must be Mr. Zain."

"Yes," he said, reaching out to shake my hand. His eyes were hidden behind sunglasses. He reminded me of an old neighbor, a man my mother didn't trust. *He's like a fox, smart and cunning,* she used to say. *He'll do anything to get what he wants. You should never trust him.*

Forcing myself to smile, I opened my purse and handed him the letter Barla had given me.

"Can I see your passport?" he asked.

Without question I handed him my passport. He looked at it and tucked it away in his briefcase. "I have to keep it with me for now. I'll give it back to you later," he promised. "Let's go."

I struggled along with my heavy suitcase, trying to keep up with his long strides, surprised he hadn't offered a helping hand. We exited the waiting area and came to the taxi stand.

"How was the flight?" he asked while we waited for a car.

"All right," I said absent-mindedly. I was worried about his holding onto my passport, but I didn't have the courage to question him.

Just then a black Mercedes pulled up in front of us. Mr. Zain opened the back door and let me in, then climbed into the seat next to me. Off the car zipped, ending my last chance to turn back and go home.

The driver reminded me of a character, Kalum, in a series of stories out of a women's weekly I had loved as a teenager. He had the same girlish face with long eyelashes and eyebrows and curly black hair. Except for his fair skin, he looked almost Sri Lankan.

For about fifteen minutes we drove through the streets of Beirut, and I kept my eyes fixed on the passing scene. Unlike the streets in Sri Lanka, these had sidewalks and were free of litter. The city was crowded with people and tall buildings and shops that looked as if they catered to the wealthy.

Presently the car stopped in front of a hotel. I followed Mr. Zain inside, past the reception area and through the restaurant, my sandals padding softly over the bright red carpet. The tables in the restaurant were black, arranged with white square tablecloths and red napkins to match the floor. A small vase with one red rose sat on each table.

One of the stewards smiled at me. On his right cheek was a black birthmark, which Sri Lankans consider a beauty mark. Without a doubt he is Sri Lankan, I said to myself, comforted by the thought. I returned his smile and padded after Mr. Zain to the elevator.

His office was on the second floor. As we entered the foyer his secretary greeted us with a smile and said something to Mr. Zain in Arabic. She signaled me to take a seat and followed Mr. Zain across the polished floor into his office, closing the doors behind her.

I wondered about the family to which I had been assigned. What would they be like? Uncertainty rekindled my fear, and suddenly a wave of exhaustion passed over me. With shaky hands, I plunked the suitcase down and collapsed on a wooden bench. The room was rectangular, with the secretary's desk at the front entrance. On the wall opposite this desk hung a painting with colorful lines going in all directions.

Presently the secretary came out of the office, smelling of perfume. Short hair framed her round face and she was tall, with a slim waist but big hips and heavy legs. As she crossed over to her desk her heavy bottom swung back and forth.

A few minutes later the curly-haired driver walked into the reception area followed by twelve Sri Lankan girls. Greatly relieved, I looked them over, and was about to ask one girl how she was faring when Mr. Zain emerged from his office. "Stand in a line," he ordered. "People are coming to get you, so smile and be pleasant."

I took my place at the end of the line and waited like a frightened deer, head down. A group of people, mostly women, breezed into the office. Like the secretary they were wearing perfume, and their high heels went *tick-tock* on the polished floor as they paced in front of us, studying our faces to discern which among us would best suit them.

So, I was wrong. I had assumed that I'd been assigned to a family, but here I was, standing in front of complete strangers like so much meat on the block. Alarmed, I kept my eyes on the floor, hoping they would go away and not choose me.

A young man in his early thirties glanced at me several times and went over to Mr. Zain. They approached me, speaking to each other in Arabic.

Do I have a say in the matter? I wondered.

Out of the corner of my eye I saw a woman hugging a girl she had just chosen. They looked like old friends. I was happy for the girl and longed for a friendly smile to ease my fears.

"Ms. Suriya, this gentleman wants to take you home to his family," Mr. Zain said, beaming like a merchant who has just made a good sale.

The gentleman turned to me. "We can go now," he said in English.

I picked up my suitcase and followed him.

"You're going to a nice family. I'm sure you'll be happy there," I heard Mr. Zain say behind me.

Without responding to him, I followed my new employer out of the hotel to his car, which seemed too big for him. He was short and had a big stomach. Thick black hair and a mustache gave him a rough appearance. He opened the back door for me and I sank into a large, cushioned leather seat. It was so deep I could hardly see where we were going. Sitting on the edge of the seat, I tried to remember any signs or landmarks on the street.

We left the busy city, came to a small town with a Catholic church on one corner, then drove toward the mountains, passing hills and valleys with sheep and goat farms.

"My name is Levi, and my wife is Beth. She'll be happy to have you," he said, looking at me through the rearview mirror.

"I hope so."

"Do you have any children?" he asked me.

"Yes, sir," I said, and tears filled my eyes at the thought of Samadha. Please let everything be all right, dear God, I wished silently.

"We have a little boy, David. He is only eight months old. You can help us take care of him."

"Yes, sir."

He did not speak again until we reached his home. It was a two-story house, far away from the city, up in the hills on a huge farm. When he parked the car in front of the house, his wife came to the door. I liked her at once. She seemed kind and greeted us with a big smile. Like Mr. Zain's secretary, she was slim above the waist with round hips and heavy legs. She must be in her early twenties, I guessed.

Beth helped me up the stairs with my suitcase. "This is your room," she said. "You must be tired. Why don't you rest now? I'll show you around later."

That sounded like music to my ears. My body ached and my stomach growled. I lay down on the bed and listened to her footsteps going down the stairs, then closed my eyes and fell into a deep sleep.

It didn't last long. Presently I became aware of a woman's figure standing by the bed. At first I thought it might be my mother because I'd been dreaming of her calling me to tea.

"You must be hungry," Beth said.

With a start, I scrambled off the bed and apologized for falling asleep.

"I'm the one who should apologize, for waking you up," she said. "Here, I brought you a sandwich."

"You're very kind. Thank you," I said.

"Why don't you eat this and go back to sleep?"

She walked over to the closet, opened the door and said, "You can use any of these clothes. Towels and blankets are in here too. Sometimes it gets a little chilly at night. You might need another blanket. If you need anything else, just ask me."

I smiled and thanked her again. When she was gone I looked around the room. It was cozy. The bed had two soft pillows and a pink blanket, and a bedside table held the tray with the sandwich and a pot of hot tea.

After eating the sandwich, which tasted like chicken and garlic, and drinking the warm, comforting tea, I began to inspect my surroundings and was happy to discover that my room had an attached bathroom and its own little balcony.

Out on the balcony it was dark, save for the stars in a wide open sky and lights from houses scattered up and down the hills. The cool air whispered and brushed past me. I searched the stars for the shape of the rosary, something we used to do at home, but no pattern took shape—they hovered far above, impersonally at random. A girl couldn't ask for a nicer room or a more considerate employer, I thought, and yet an unbearable sense of loneliness overwhelmed me.

I woke at dawn, my strength restored. All I needed was a quick shower to start the day. Never in my life had I had the luxury of my own room or an attached bathroom. This is a good start, I thought, coming out of the shower.

Dressed in a pink skirt and a short-sleeved blouse my mother had made me, I ventured out of my room, downstairs and into the front yard, where a baby lamb played with its mother. The sun was still hidden behind the hills, and everyone in the house was asleep. It seemed like a good time to check the closet, so I went back to my room and sifted through the clothes. Inside hung a row of beautiful dresses. A purple velvet robe, soft and silky to the touch, with an embroidered collar, caught my eye. I tried it on but it was too long for me, and the dresses didn't fit any better.

Suddenly a cry pierced the silence, and instinctively I dropped the robe and ran to the source, thinking for an instant that it was my son. The baby was sitting in his crib crying; when he saw me his sobs just grew louder. I picked him up and tried to comfort him, cooing and talking gently. He was heavy, much heavier than Samadha had been at eight months, and his round chubby face was red and wet. With a towel from the nearby rack I wiped his face. He stopped crying and stared at me, lower lip shivering, not knowing whether to break into cries again. I tickled his stomach and made him laugh.

Soon Beth came into the room. "Oh!" she exclaimed, surprised. "You're up already."

"Yes, I woke up early."

"I see you've met David. He always wakes up early. He needs his bottle now," she said, heading to the kitchen to prepare the bottle. I followed along.

"I'm going back to bed. Could you watch the baby for a little while?" she asked.

"Yes, madam."

After he had his bottle I took David to his room and played with him for a couple of hours. The room was filled with expensive toys—a flying airplane, a bear playing a drum set, musical animals—and I was struck that he knew how to play with them. What would Samadha do if he had all of these toys? I wondered. Perhaps my mother would put them all in the living room cabinet to keep them from breaking.

Beth, who was up by now, called me into the kitchen and showed me how to set the table for their breakfast. A pot of tea with sugar and milk, fruit, toasted pita bread and butter and jam were all they had in the morning.

"My sister-in-law lives on the first floor. They also have a Sri Lankan maid," Beth said.

I was happy to hear that and thought we would be able to get together when we had free time. "When can I meet her?" I asked.

"Oh, they have lots of parties. When they do they'll need your help and you'll get to meet her then," said Beth.

"Can't I see her today?" I asked.

"No, I don't think my sister-in-law would like that."

I decided to be patient. Just the thought of another Sri Lankan living close by was comforting.

Beth pointed to another house on the same land. "Levi's parents live in that house, and when they have visitors she might need your help."

So I would be working for three families for one salary. At least it would not be every day.

Beth took me through the house, showed me where everything was and explained my duties. It was a nice little home on the second floor: three bedrooms, a living room, a kitchen, two baths and a small storage room.

"You need to vacuum the rooms every day," Beth said as she pulled a vacuum cleaner from the storage room.

"Please, show me how it works," I said awkwardly. It was the very first time I had seen such a thing and I marveled at the way the machine sucked up dust and bits of debris, which made tiny clinks and clacks as it passed into the bag. It was so much easier to vacuum a carpeted floor than to mop a cement or wooden floor.

Beth gave me a long list of chores to complete before the day's end. Starting with the bedrooms, I changed the sheets, dusted the furniture and vacuumed, then I moved on to the living room and dusted and mopped. The most disagreeable of my morning duties was cleaning the bathrooms. The windows were to be washed once a week.

So much physical labor was new to me, and my body began to ache all over.

"I need your help in here," Beth called out, and I joined her in the kitchen to help cook lunch. I ate alone in the kitchen. After the family meal was over I cleared the table, cleaned the pots and pans and washed the kitchen floor.

My afternoon was mostly spent washing and ironing clothes. In between chores Beth asked me to watch David, which was a welcome change. I loved being around him.

That night I fell into bed without a shower, completely spent. There was no strength left in my body to write to my parents, and for the first time I understood the hardship of a servant's life. Within a few days, however, I became accustomed to the work and was able to finish more chores with fewer breaks.

Every now and then I went over to help Levi's mother with her housework. She was old, her head covered with a few gray hairs pinned together at the nape of her neck. Unlike her son, she was pleasant and spoke to me kindly. Settling her heavy body on the soft couch, she offered me food. "Have some sweets, these are very good," she would say, then send me to her kitchen to make tea. After the little treat, she would fall asleep on the couch, leaving me to my work.

The work kept me busy and the days sped by, but loneliness engulfed me. Three weeks passed and there was no news from my parents. Why weren't they writing to me? Impatiently, I waited. Every night before going to bed I listened to my son's voice on a tape and dashed off a few lines to him. Beth said I was not allowed to go outdoors, so once a week I handed Levi a letter to mail to my family.

One day while cleaning Beth's bedroom I found some hairpins on the table, opened the drawer to put them away and spotted the letters I'd given to Levi to mail to my parents. My heart sank. Without letters from me, how would my parents know where to write? My first instinct was to confront Levi and Beth, but they were my employers; how dare I question them? Beth would think I had been going through her drawers. Best to give it some thought and find a proper way to question them, I decided, putting the letters back in the drawer and continuing with my work. I had to find a way to contact my parents. My only hope was to speak with the maid at Levi's sister's.

Later that week Beth took me down to her sister-in-law's house on the first floor.

"We're having a party today and we could use your help with the cooking," Beth said as she showed me into her sister-in-law's kitchen.

In spite of the extra work, I was pleased finally to meet the other Sri Lankan.

"Marli, this is Ranga," Beth said, introducing me to the maid. "She's going to help you."

Marli was at the kitchen sink washing dishes. She greeted me with a smile, handed me a towel to dry the dishes and went on working without a word.

"Have you been here long?" I asked her.

"Six months," she whispered.

Sensing her fear, I lowered my voice. "Are they good to you?"

She looked over her shoulder before answering. "Yes, but I'll be in trouble if she sees me talking to you."

"Why?"

"She's a mean woman; she doesn't want us to be friends. She told me not to have any contact with you."

"But we're from the same country, all alone here, and we work for the same family. What is wrong with us being friends?"

She shrugged her shoulders and kept quiet. I didn't want to be quiet; there were many questions to ask her. For weeks I had waited for a chance to speak with her, and I had to make the most of it.

"Do you write to your family?" I asked her softly.

"Yes."

"Do you hear from them?"

"Yes, don't you hear from yours?"

"I found all my letters in Levi's desk. He's not mailing my letters. There's no way for my parents to know where I am without my letters."

"Oh! That man is just like his sister, very mean," she said.

I saw my chance and asked her, "Can you mail one of my letters? Your parents can mail it to my parents."

"I don't know, Ranga; I don't want to get into trouble."

"Can you at least send them a message through your parents?"

Before she could answer, a woman came into the kitchen and barked, "Stop talking and do your work!"

I turned around and saw a young woman with a small baby face and rosy cheeks hovering in the doorway. Black curly hair clustered over her shoulders.

Ignoring her anger, I smiled at her and said, "I'm Ranga."

"I know who you are! You're here to help and that's all. I don't want to hear you two whispering," and off she stormed.

Marli looked like a baby deer; her eyes filled with tears and she moved away from me to peel potatoes. Helplessly I stared at her, thinking how lucky I was to have Beth as my employer. Marli and I didn't talk to each other for the rest of the day.

We heard the cry of the sheep as Levi and his brother-in-law pulled it down to the ground and cut its throat. It was Marli's and my very first time seeing an animal slaughtered. She got sick to her stomach watching the blood pouring down its neck while it shivered. The innocent eyes were still open as they took the skin off its head. They hung it on a tree, skinned and cleaned it, then cooked it on the fire.

It was a day of feasting, a family gathering, but I had no idea what they were celebrating. There was a big crowd and they all had fun drinking and dancing. Marli and I served them food and watched them enjoying their feast. Neither of us tasted that meat. It was a long, tiring day for both of us.

Sunday was my day off, and though I was an Adventist I wanted to go to a Catholic church. I had heard that mass was the best place to meet other Sri Lankan maids.

That night I asked Beth if I could go to the Catholic church on Sunday.

"We can't let you go anywhere alone," she replied, "and we don't go to the Catholic church but we'll take you to our church." So the following Sunday Beth and Levi took me to their church, a Protestant church of some sort.

That was the last time I went to church. I spent Sundays in my room and sometimes took care of David.

One morning during my fifth week, I didn't wake up at my usual time. When I did wake up my body felt weak and cold even under two blankets. I was still in bed when Beth knocked on the door. As I tried to get up, I felt dizzy and everything around me started spinning.

"Are you all right?" Beth asked.

"I don't feel good, madam." She came close to me and I felt her cold palm on my forehead.

"You're burning up. You'd better stay in bed; don't worry about the work."

For three days I stayed in bed while Beth brought me soup and toast. On the fourth day I felt better and resumed my regular work. That afternoon I was taking a little break when Beth came into my room.

"You have to get dressed and get your bag ready," she said. "Levi is coming for you."

"Where am I going?" I asked.

She looked at me with a worried expression. "I'm sorry, Ranga. Hurry and get dressed," she said, and left the room without an explanation.

Alarmed, I scrambled to get dressed and pack my bag. Levi came to the door and I followed him downstairs to a waiting taxi.

"Where are you sending me?" I asked Levi. "Aren't you coming with me?"

"This taxi will take you to Mr. Zain," he said.

"Why? Did I do something wrong? Can I please talk to Beth?"

"We don't want you anymore," he said, slamming the door.

Before I could say anything else, the taxi took off.

Now what's going to happen to me? I thought. As far as I knew, aside from being sick, I had done everything right, but for some unknown reason they didn't need me anymore and they hadn't paid me anything for the month I had worked for them. At the same time I was almost relieved. This might be my chance to go to a good home where I would be free to mail my letters and have friends.

The driver must have taken a different road going back to the city because I didn't recognize anything on the street. He drove in silence; I tried to talk to him but he didn't understand English.

Once we were out of the mountains he stopped the car next to a park, turned to me and rattled off something in Arabic. I thought he was asking me for Mr. Zain's address, but I didn't have his address or the telephone number with me. When I tried to explain that he had to take me to Mr. Zain, he got out of the car, yanked the suitcase from the trunk and signaled for me to get out. When I hesitated, he grabbed my hand and pulled me out. Muttering a few words in Arabic, he climbed back in, slammed the door and drove off, leaving me all alone.

Chapter 3

As the taxi disappeared into the traffic, I stood rooted to the ground, numb with fear. Slowly the noises around me started to register, as if I were emerging from a state of unconsciousness—horns blaring, leaves rustling, the voices of people passing by and the laughter of children playing in the park. Huge trees, their branches reaching out to neighboring trees, created a canopy over the street.

The sunlight began to fade. People everywhere were hurrying home to their loved ones. A young couple strolled by, locked in an embrace. Everything seemed normal to everyone else. No one noticed me.

Soon it would be dark and I had to find shelter. I had no money to go to a hotel and no idea how to find Mr. Zain. I picked up my suitcase, shivering, tears blurring my vision. A few yards ahead of me the street was divided. Which path should I take? Whom should I ask for help? My only hope was to find a policeman. Please help me, God, I heard myself repeating, please help me, God. My legs picked up the rhythm of the chant and kept me moving.

After about a quarter of a mile a woman appeared a few yards ahead, her eyes focused on me. She wore brown pants with a beige silk shirt and a soft print scarf around her neck. A hat covered her head. There was something about her that seemed familiar. I ignored her as we passed, but turned around to take another look. She turned around too and we faced each other. She had a round pretty face that didn't need any makeup. With a curious expression, she asked, "Are you lost?"

"No," I said hesitantly, and started walking.

I didn't know whom to trust anymore. I heard her footsteps coming after me and I whirled around. "I'm Padma," she said in Sinhalese. "Are you from Sri Lanka?"

Her fair skin and modern dress had fooled me. "Yes," I nodded.

"Are you in any kind of trouble?" she asked. The concern in her voice broke down my fears. She held my hand and moved me to the side of the street. "Please don't be afraid. Tell me what happened, I'll help you any way I can."

Comforted by her words, I asked her, "Can you take me to a police station?"

"Why do you need to go to the police? What happened?"

I explained to her briefly what had happened, and she was surprised. "I hear these stories every day—it's hard to believe anyone could do this to another human being!" She paused. "I know Mr. Zain, I can take you to him."

I let out a deep sigh of relief. "Can you take me to him now?" I pleaded.

"The office will be closed now and tomorrow is a holiday, so you'll have to wait until the day after."

"How could they do this to me? What am I going to do now?"

"Don't worry, you can stay with me," she said.

"Are you working for a family?"

"Yes, but they are very nice people."

"Won't they be mad if you take me there?"

"No, I don't live with them. I have my own room; I'm free to do anything I want."

It was the best news I had heard for a long time; I was glad that I could be myself for one whole day. She took me to her room, a small annex with one bedroom, a kitchen and a bathroom. We spent the night talking. The next day she took me outdoors to show me around, then cooked a wonderful Sri Lankan meal—chicken curry and rice.

"You don't have to go to Mr. Zain. I can put you in a good home," she said.

"My passport is with Mr. Zain."

"That's not a problem. The family I'm going to place you with can contact Mr. Zain and get your passport."

It was a tempting offer, but I believed it would be safer to keep the connection with Mr. Zain, so I decided to go back to the agency.

That night I thanked God for watching over me and asked for his guidance and further protection.

When Padma took me to Mr. Zain, he didn't look surprised to see me. "There you are," he said, as if nothing had happened. Padma explained to him how she had met me.

"What would have happened if Padma hadn't helped me?" I said. "How could they send me away like that? Aren't they responsible for what happens to me?"

Mr. Zain gave me a penetrating look, threatening me silently. Then he smiled. "Nothing happened to you, so why worry about it? Aren't you safe now?"

His answer destroyed my confidence in him. I knew then that I was alone and he was not to be trusted if I was ever in trouble. There was no sense arguing with him. He would always side with his clients. I decided to take precautions.

"Can I have your telephone number and address, in case I get lost again?" I asked. He took out a business card and gave it to me.

Padma and I went out into the reception area to say goodbye. I copied Mr. Zain's address and phone number onto a letter I had written my parents and gave it to her. "Please mail this." She hugged me and said, "Don't be afraid, now you have me. If you ever get into trouble, take a taxi and come to my room or call me." She handed me twenty Lebanese pounds. "Keep this for an emergency." I thanked her over and over again and held onto her hand, wanting her to stay a little longer.

After she had gone I went back to Mr. Zain's office to await my destiny.

"You went to a good family. Why did you have to fake being sick?" Mr. Zain asked.

Incredulous, I stared at him. "Fake being sick?"

"Weren't you?"

"Is that what they told you? How can I fake a fever? How can I fake dizziness?" Anger was boiling inside me, but the look on his face said he didn't believe me.

"I have enough experience with the tricks you girls play on us. Don't pretend to be so innocent."

I kept quiet and didn't look at him when he spoke to me again.

"Until I can find a new home for you I will have to put you in a hotel, and you will have to pay the bill once you start working."

"Can't you send me back home?" I asked hopefully.

"Do you have the money to pay back the ticket fare?"

So that was the deal. Even if I did have the money to cover the airfare, I sensed, he wouldn't send me back until the contract was over. Going home was not an option. Summoning up my courage, I said, "Who's going to pay me for the time I worked for Beth? They didn't pay me."

"I'll give them a call and get that money for you. Now go and stay in the reception area until I find someone to take you to the hotel."

As I was leaving his office, the other door opened and a tall skinny woman walked in wearing a dark blue suit, a red jacket and a red hat. She walked purposefully over to the secretary, exchanged some words with her, then turned around and stared at me. Her face was slathered with makeup; her eyes looked big and black from too much mascara.

She went into Mr. Zain's office and I heard their voices. A few minutes later they appeared in the reception area. Giving me another hard look, she came closer and placed her long fingernail under my chin.

"Hello there, pretty one. I'm Lisha and you're coming home with me, girl. Aren't you glad?" She walked over to the secretary without waiting for my response.

"It's your lucky day, Ms. Suriya. This nice lady would like to take you to her home," said Mr. Zain.

I knew I wouldn't stand a chance if I refused to go with her, but I asked him anyway, in a whisper. "Can I go to another home, Mr. Zain? I'm not comfortable going with her."

He must have sensed my discomfort. "Don't worry," he replied softly. "She's a nice lady, a very rich woman. You should be happy to go with her."

His words didn't allay my fear, but there was no use trying to reason with him, so I kept quiet. After she had signed all the papers I followed her out of the building to her big white car. She let me sit in front with her and drove off as if her back was on fire.

"Are you married?" she asked.

"Yes, madam," I said, without going into details.

"Do you have children?"

"Yes, one."

"How old?"

"He's three years old."

"Well, if you stay with me I can bring your husband and the child to live with you."

"That would be nice, madam," I said, not believing it.

"I'm rich, I have the money to do anything I want. So you be good and I'll help you."

We drove farther from the city, the ocean to our right. This area was completely different from the mountainside. The streets, though busy and lined with many buildings, were wide and clean, and trees along the road shaded the sidewalks. It was somewhat comforting knowing I was close to the city.

She pulled into a luxury condominium complex with meticulous landscaping and flowerbeds hugging the driveway. Parking was on the ground floor. Guards stood at the entrance. We got out of the car, took the elevator to the fourth floor, and with that swift introduction I began my new life.

It was a beautiful condo, a semicircular layout taking up the entire fourth floor. When I stepped into the family room I felt out of place; my old shoes looked ugly against the marble floor. The brick walls, vaulted ceiling and overstuffed furniture screamed wealth. There were floor-to-ceiling windows and gill-shaped concrete slabs in front of each window to protect the glass from the wind. The family room faced the main entrance.

"This is the only entrance," Lisha said. "It's where the children hang out, watch TV and have their meals. You need to keep this area very clean."

"You have children?" I asked, wondering how much extra work there would be with children around.

"Didn't I tell you? I have two girls and one boy. Their father works in Dubai. He comes home only for the holidays."

"How old are they?" I asked.

"Well, let me think. Deanna is twelve; Jamal, my darling boy, is eight; and Jena is six. You'll meet them tonight," she said, and went on with her instructions about the daily cleaning.

Fanned out of the family room from left to right were the living room, dining room, kitchen, four bedrooms, and a study. There was an elegant wraparound balcony with sliding glass doors leading from each room for easy access outside. We went into the living room, roomy and over furnished with antiques and rich upholstery. The polished wooden floor gave way to lush carpet in the sitting area. There were three cabinets, one each for china, silver and brassware. Two breathtaking chandeliers with five tiers of crystal graced the ceiling.

She walked over to the china cabinet. "You have to open the cabinets and dust and clean everything inside before you vacuum and mop the floors."

I nodded, wondering how I would ever finish all this cleaning in a single day.

Each child's bedroom was carpeted, with a floor-to-ceiling glass wall facing the balcony and a study area for the occupant. Lisha had a sumptuous, lavishly decorated master bedroom suite with a walk-in closet.

The kitchen was spacious and full of appliances, with a terrazzo floor, ceramic counters and custom cabinetry.

My room was in between the kitchen and the dining room, alongside the laundry room and with a separate bathroom. The room was small, no windows or access to the balcony, with a twin bed, closet, nightstand and bureau. The only entrance to the room was through the kitchen. One look at the room and I felt trapped.

The condo was huge, as was the amount of work I was expected to do each day, which made the workload at Beth's look like play. I consoled myself by thinking that at least I knew *how* to do housework, having been trained at my former employer's.

After the house tour Lisha went to get her children from school. I walked around the balcony observing the breathtaking view. A six-foot brick wall surrounded the building and grounds, which were filled with plants and manicured flowerbeds. All around, as far as the eye could see, were buildings of different sizes and shapes filled the whole town.

That afternoon I helped Lisha with the dinner. After instructing me how to set the children's table in the family room, she put my plate on the kitchen table and said, "I'd like for you to wait until the children are done with their meals."

After dinner I was introduced to her children. Deanna was tall and slim with short hair and a full figure that belied her age. She smiled at me when I said hello. Jamal was big, round and muscular. Jena was just like her mother, thin with long hair down to her waist. She looked at me out of the corner of her eye, then ignored me completely.

After I had my dinner and cleaned up the kitchen, Deanna asked me to join them watching TV, and I did.

There was a chair for me behind the sofas. I sat there for a little while feeling like an extra piece of furniture.

My day began at five in the morning. Wearing a white uniform Lisha had given me, I reached for the list. My first chore was to water the plants on the balcony before sunrise. Then I cleaned the family room, prepared breakfast and set the table. Once the children were gone I went into their bedrooms, which were a mess. It took me an eternity to straighten them out. Jamal had wet his bed and his room smelled urine. By the time I was done with the bedrooms, it was way past lunchtime. I had no time to spare for breaks, so I kept on with my chores into the evening, cleaning the living room, dining room, kitchen and balcony. Not only did I have to clean the windows and glass doors that were all over the house, but also had I to wash and mop all of the cement floors, including the balcony.

Lisha hadn't provided me with gloves. When I asked for some, she said, "Why do you need gloves? Gloves won't help you with your chores." So I had to do all my cleaning without them, even the toilets.

It was past midnight when I finally went to bed with an aching body and swollen fingers.

The next day, Lisha came home while I was cleaning her room. I hadn't yet vacuumed the floor, and when she bent to look under the bed she started yelling at me for the dust there. "I haven't had a chance—" I started to explain, but she cut me off.

"You filthy brat, don't you ever argue with me!"

Alarmed at her behavior, I decided to choose my words with more care in the future. After she left I bent over and looked under the bed. I couldn't tell whether it was vacuumed or not.

A couple of days later I was doing the laundry when I saw some underwear in the sink with bloodstains. I tossed them into the washing machine along with the other clothes. Presently Lisha came into the laundry room in her favorite red robe, looking like a ghost without her makeup.

"Where are the panties I put in the sink?" she demanded. I knew I was in trouble even before I answered her.

"I put them with the other clothes in the machine," I said. Her eyes widened and her face turned red, and out of the blue she twisted my ear and shoved me toward the washing machine.

"Take them out now and wash them with your hands!"

I opened the lid to the machine and located the underwear. She pulled me back to the sink and turned on the hot water.

"Now wash them, rub the stains with your fingers and don't use any cold water."

What is wrong with this woman, is she crazy? I thought, silently following her instructions. My fingers were already sore from all the cleaning I'd been doing, and as I rubbed the panties against my raw skin, it started to peel. With the soap and hot water it felt as if someone were slicing my fingers with a knife. Rolling my eyes, I sucked the tears back and bit my lip to control the pain. After she was gone I put my fingers in cold water and cried.

As my time at Lisha's continued, I tried to do my best to stay out of trouble. I saw the children only at dinner and they were no trouble, but their rooms were disasters. Lisha spent most of her day away from home, which gave me peace to do my chores. I didn't know where she went or whether she had a job, nor did I ask. She always left the house with the children, some days she dropped by the house during mid-afternoon for an hour or so, then left again. She always came home with the children late afternoon.

I woke up crying one morning. In my dream Samadha had been kidnapped by Tilak. Hearing his cries, I went searching for him and discovered that he had been locked up in a room in my mother-in-law's home. I climbed through the window and was running toward Samadha when Tilak burst into the room, grabbed him and ran off.

I felt better knowing it was only a dream, but I couldn't help wondering if it had really happened. I hadn't heard from my parents yet, and it killed me not knowing for sure that my son was safe. With a heavy heart, I got ready to start another long day. As I brushed my hair I softly sang his favorite lullaby, wishing he could hear it in his dreams.

My heart cannot bear the love I feel for you;
I am your Amma, my dear son,
I want to kiss your cheeks and hold you in my arms,
This is a wish of an unfortunate mother.

Suddenly I saw Lisha standing next to me. I hadn't heard her come in and had no time to wipe my tears and put on a smile. She grabbed the brush out of my hand and struck my face with it. It took me by surprise and for a second I thought it was a dream, until I felt a stinging pain as the bristles dug into my flesh.

"Why are you hitting me?" I asked, covering my eyes from her attacks.

She kept hitting me again and again, aiming for my eyes. Finally the brush broke in her hand and she punched me in the nose.

"I give you shelter, I give you food, there is no reason for you to cry! This is not the way to start your day!" she screamed.

I was speechless. I had learned very young never to cry in front of anyone, but I always felt free to cry when I was alone.

"I will kill you if I ever catch you crying in this house. Now wash up and start your work in the living room. Do not go to the family room until the children are gone." She departed just the way she came in, without a sound.

As I gazed in the mirror and saw the swelling above my left eyebrow and the bruises on my face, I wondered if she was mentally ill. One thing was sure—she didn't want the children to know that I had been hurt.

It was clear that I would have to be even more careful with this woman. I remembered Padma and thought of calling her, but when I went to use the phone—the only one she had in the condo, an outdated rotary phone—it was locked. I tried to open the door to go down to the first floor and ask the guards if I could use their phone, but it too was locked. So, she had thought of everything.

Lisha didn't come home until late that evening, nor had she left me any breakfast or lunch. I didn't dare touch any food without her permission.

When I sat down to my dinner that night, I looked down on leftovers from the children's plates: half-eaten flatbread and chicken skin and bones with a little meat left on the edges. I felt like a beggar from the streets, but my hunger surpassed my pride and I ate every scrap I could find, washing it down with water.

I fell into bed, hungry, hurt and frightened, and prayed all night, asking God to show me a way out of this misery. I thought of my father, whom I believed had psychic and mystical powers. He claimed that he could feel and see things without being present physically. Can't you see my suffering? I wondered. Can't you use your power to help me?

Chapter 4

After the hairbrush incident, not a single day went by without a knock on the head, a squeeze of the ear, a slap on the face or verbal abuse. Day after day, week after week, Lisha found an excuse to hit me. It could be something as simple as a spot that she thought I hadn't cleaned, or a dying plant. She didn't need a reason to hit me. Lisha breathed energy into her own life by abusing me.

With every passing day I became more miserable, and more obsessed with finding a way out. First I started to write down everything in a diary. Then I tried to look for help. When I was on the balcony I kept my eyes on the road, hoping to see someone walking by. I had no idea who occupied the other three floors in the building and didn't see anyone on the grounds, but I didn't give up. I learned to be alert and watchful.

Once a girl appeared on the balcony of another building few blocks away and frantically I waved to her, hoping she was a maid. She saw me, but just turned around and disappeared inside.

I wrote a note and carried it in my uniform pocket, hoping to give it to someone if there was ever a chance. *Please help me, I am in danger*, it said, and underneath this message my name appeared, along with Padma's and Mr. Zain's telephone numbers.

Late one afternoon Lisha decided to take me shopping with her. That was the first time I had been allowed out of the house in three weeks. I didn't know what made her feel like taking me outdoors, but I was glad.

"I need to buy you a dress," she said. I was startled. Maybe she felt guilty for abusing me. Was she trying to make up for it by getting me a dress? It didn't matter to me one way or the other. Nothing she did could excuse her treatment of me.

She drove into the city, parked the car, lit a cigarette and walked with me along the sidewalk. The roads were busy and the shops crowded. Anxiety was rising inside me. I wanted to run away, to get lost in the crowd. A voice inside me said *Run, run*, but I had to do it right. I had to wait for the perfect chance. Lisha pulled me into a clothing store, staying right behind me like a shadow and covering me with her cigarette smoke.

"Could you help find her a dress?" Lisha asked a salesgirl. The salesgirl must have sensed the tension between us because she kept glancing at our faces as she walked us through the clothes stands. Presently she plucked a dress from the rack, held it up and said, "This would look nice on you. Why don't you try it on?"

That gave me an idea, and I smiled at her. While I was in the fitting room trying on the dress, the salesgirl waited outside with Lisha. I put the dress on quickly, took out my note and waited. When the salesgirl peeked in between the curtains, I signaled her to come in.

"Please help me," I said, and just as I was about to hand over the note and explain what to do with it, Lisha barged in. She looked at both of us with her eagle eyes, trying to figure out what was going on.

"I'll buy this dress—it looks good on her," Lisha said, putting her hand on my shoulder and guiding me over to the counter. I walked out of that store feeling lost. When I glanced back I saw the salesgirl talking with the other girls, and they all had their eyes on me. By the looks on their faces I could tell they knew something was wrong.

Lisha picked her children up at school and dropped us off at the beach. "Stay close to the children," she said. "I'll be right back," and she was gone.

I couldn't tell if the children knew their mother was abusing me. Whenever she hit me, Lisha made sure we were alone in the house or in my room, out of sight. The kids hardly ever saw me. Once Deanna noticed the bruise on my forehead and stared at me, but she didn't say anything.

After all that time being under lock and key, closely watched by Lisha, here I was alone with the children for a while. They ran into the water and I ran after them, taking off my slippers and wading in. The water felt warm on my bare feet. The wind was cool and sticky and I thought how good it was to be free. Deanna and Jamal began strolling along the beach a few yards ahead of me, with Jena trailing behind them. Slowly I started to veer toward the road; they didn't see me walking away from them, and all of a sudden I broke into a run.

"Where are you going?" Jena called. "My mother said to stay with us!"

I turned around and saw her right behind me, her mean eyes just like her mother's, filled with disgust. I was upset but how could I hate her—she was only a child.

"I need to find a bathroom," I lied.

"You have to wait until my mother gets here," she demanded. Just then I saw Lisha walking toward us. She drove us back home, back to my prison.

I came up with many plans to escape. One was climbing down the balcony wall. The bricks protruded about an inch from the wall, creating narrow stairs all the way to the ground. Surely the bricks would hold my small feet if I could find a rope to hold onto while going down, I thought. There wasn't a long enough rope in the house so I decided to use my three saris, each six yards long. It would be risky, but I had to try.

After everyone had gone to bed that night, I tied the saris together and slipped onto the balcony. Over in the corner, I tied one end of my makeshift rope to the railing and let the rest of it dangle in the air. It was dark, but the lights in the yard illuminated the area. After making sure no one was around, I climbed over the railing, gripping the sari and groping for a brick to place my foot on. Alas, the gap between each protruding brick was too great, and my short legs couldn't even reach the first one. It was a chilly night but I was sweating from fear of falling. After climbing back onto the balcony I returned to my room, weighed down by a sense of hopeless defeat.

In addition to shouldering a tremendous load of work and suffering abuse, I was being starved. When Lisha continued to serve me leftovers from the children's plates, I realized that it wasn't absent-minded on her part, it was deliberate. Knowing it could be my only meal for the day, I swallowed anything that was served to me. Some days I even went through the kitchen trash, scrabbling around for something to eat and filling my stomach with fish bones and chewed food.

One day I was so weak that I made a cup of tea when Lisha wasn't around, and while fixing it I recalled a scene from my childhood. I must have been about three or four years old. My parents were very poor then and I hadn't had anything to eat the whole day. My stomach was growling. I went to Menica, a teenager who lived with us, and asked her if she would make me some tea.

She glanced at me sadly and said, "There's no tea in the house, Chuty baby."

"Can't you make some with water, Menica?"

She picked me up, carried me to the neighbor's house and knocked on the kitchen door. A woman came out. She was the woman who squeezed my cheeks whenever she saw me. I buried my face against Menica's shoulder to keep my cheeks from being pinched.

"Hello, Chuty baby, are you going for a walk with Menica?" she asked, pulling my curls instead.

Menica didn't wait for me to answer. "*Nona*," which meant madam, "we have some visitors in the house and I ran out of tea. I don't have time to run to the store right now. Can I please borrow some?"

I didn't understand then why Menica had to lie, but thanks to her that afternoon I drank some tea and filled my empty stomach.

The memory strengthened me. I had survived hunger as a child and I would survive it now. After all these years, a cup of tea still filled my stomach.

Another week went by and nothing changed; the abuse continued. I began searching the condo for keys to the door. Each day I waited for Lisha to leave the house, and each day after she left I resumed my methodical hunt, looking in every drawer and cabinet I could open. Finally a set of keys showed up on the telephone stand in the family room. Heart pounding, I ran to the door. One by one I tried the keys, my hand shaking. At last, I thought, as the final key on the chain slid into the hole—freedom at last! But it wouldn't turn. I pulled it and pushed it and jiggled it to no avail. And so I began to apply pressure, more and more pressure, turning as hard as I could until the shaft simply snapped off.

"Oh, my God, why is this happening to me?" I cried out loud, staring down at the jagged shard of metal in my hand. What was I going to do now? Lisha would kill me this time. Trembling with fear, I dashed into the kitchen, took out two steak knives and returned to the door. I inserted the knife tips into the hole where the broken piece was wedged and tried to pull it out. It was difficult to get a grip—one or the other knife kept slipping out—but finally, many long minutes later, I succeeded in extracting the key. Relief flooded over me as I collapsed on the floor, bathed in sweat. When I recovered, my first instinct was to hide the broken key or throw it into the trash chute. It soon occurred to me that that wouldn't do any good. When she found out the key was missing she would blame me. It seemed more prudent to leave the keys where I found them. Perhaps she wouldn't see them for a couple of days. Delayed punishment was all I could hope for.

For the rest of the day, all I could think about what Lisha was going to do to me—how she was going to hit me, with what and for how long. The more I waited, the more frightened I grew. The hunger, the exhaustion, all the feelings that were a normal part of my day vanished, overtaken by fear. No matter how hard I tried I couldn't come up with an excuse for what I had been doing with the key.

Finally she came home. Every time I heard her footsteps my breathing stopped. She waited until the children went to bed to confront me. I was in the kitchen cleaning dishes when she stormed in, holding the broken key on her extended palm. She slapped me with the other hand.

"Can you explain to me what you were doing with my car keys?" she asked.

They were only her car keys! I stood there speechless.

"Did you think you could run away from me, you rotten, stupid brat? Do you think I'm that stupid?" Then she slapped me until my cheeks were numb.

"I am going to teach you a lesson that you will never forget," she said, and left the kitchen. A few minutes later she came back with the guard. He was dressed like a policeman with a rifle in his hand.

"Take a good look at this girl," she said to the guard. "If you ever see her out of this house, shoot her. You have my permission."

I looked at him. I couldn't read his thoughts but heard him say, "Yes, madam."

After he was gone, Lisha grabbed me by my hair and dragged me to my room. She pushed me down and kicked me, then raised my head and banged it on the floor, muttering in Arabic all the while. I tried to fight back, tried to protect myself, but she was too strong for me. When I finally gave in, she kicked me again and spat on me. Then in a flash she was gone.

I lay on the floor, my head bursting with pain; my ribs felt as if they were broken. I had no strength to get up so I lay there for a long time in a pool of blood. I had two big bumps on my head and one was slightly cracked. At last I collected myself, crawled into the bathroom and soaked my body in hot water.

The image of the guard with his rifle in hand stirred up memories of the 1971 war in Sri Lanka, when government officials would capture innocent youths and torture them violently. I felt as if I was one of them now, wrongly accused, tortured and put in a prison. A crushing, dehumanizing sense of powerlessness fell over me.

The next morning I dragged myself out of bed, weak, aching and exhausted after a sleepless night, and got to work. The next four weeks felt like a hundred years. As the abuse continued I grew progressively weaker, and as I grew weaker I needed more time to complete my tasks. The days became longer and the nights shorter. No matter how hard I tried to sleep with the little time I had, my aching body kept me up all night. Hope dwindled, a sputtering flame about to go out. I called out to God but God seemed beyond reach.

Standing on the sill, I was cleaning the open windows. One tiny slip and I would fall, four floors down, and splatter onto the concrete pavement. For a split second, I was tempted to let go. It would look like an accident. My parents will get a settlement and they'll take care of my son, I thought. Then I remembered the innocent, sad face of dear Samadha—I didn't want to die! For his sake, I couldn't give up just yet. If I died I would never see him again, and he would be alone in this world. Then again, what proof did I have that I would ever get out of this place alive? I looked down again at the concrete pavement. No, I was not ready to kill myself. Samadha gave me the strength to go on.

That afternoon, I wracked my brain to come up with a better plan of escape, and an idea came to me—to act as if I had gone crazy. Maybe she would want to get rid of me if she thought something was wrong. Indeed, I must have been out of my mind to think I could pull it off.

The next morning just before Lisha woke up, I went to the family room with my hair all messed up. I began to make noises, yelled and banged on the furniture. Presently Lisha appeared, coming straight at me, her face steaming with anger; she grabbed me by the hair and hit me.

"You want to be crazy? I can make you crazy," she said, and pulled me near the wall and banged my head against it. She didn't stop until I gave up my act. "You think you can outsmart me, stupid bitch? If you try any of these tricks with me again, you don't want to know what I will do to you."

I asked for it that time. Ashamed of my own stupidity, I ran to the bathroom, my makeshift hospital. When I held my head under the cold water, I felt dizzy and nauseous.

As the weeks turned into months, Lisha's sprawling, luxurious condo became my cell. The screen doors and windows laughed, and the locked doors mocked me.

She never took me outdoors again. Without a word from my parents or the agency, I concluded that the letters I had been writing my family were not being mailed, and without any contact with the outside world, it seemed like a mirage. For me, the world beyond my cell did not exist.

The sun that lighted Lisha's world left mine in the dark. I watched the moon at night, wishing it could take a message to my parents. Still there was no sign of God. Facing each day became a huge challenge. How could I function without hope?

Gradually, I turned into a machine. My body stopped feeling the pain and I had no tears left to cry. My eyes got used to sleepless nights, and visions of food satisfied my hunger. I was tuned into Lisha's behavior—heard her ghostly footsteps before she walked, heard her harsh voice before she spoke, felt her cold hand before she struck.

The future was a blank, the present a terror. The past was all I had to keep me alive. Somehow the memory of my son at the airport with his innocent baby face lingered in my mind. Every second of every day his face flashed before my eyes, and I embraced it to find the courage to go on.

Helplessly, I thought of my parents. For loving and caring for me, what had I given them? Nothing but broken promises, disappointments, shame and suffering. Why hadn't I listened to them and studied hard and become somebody, instead of running away with a man? Though I had once hated living with my parents, now I missed my home desperately. The ache of guilt was greater than the physical abuse I suffered. One more time I prayed to the God who was all but invisible, and this time I said, "Please give me another chance to go back home, to ask my parents' forgiveness and to be an obedient daughter to them. I promise you, Lord, I'll make them happy."

At the end of another long and tiring day, I stood under the shower trying to comfort my aching body as the warm water caressed my bruises. Wrapping a towel around my wet hair and covering myself with another, I came out of the bathroom and walked toward my room.

Suddenly my heart stopped. Lisha's big dark eyes were glaring at me. She was standing in the doorway, blocking the entrance to my room. Her hands on her waist, face red with rage, she ground her teeth and smirked.

What have I done now? I thought, frozen in front of her. She took a step forward, grabbed me by the shoulder and laughed, like a cat playing with its victim before the kill.

"Where is it? Tell me now before I break your arm."

"What are you looking for, madam?" I said.

"Don't play games with me. I know you stole it, so hand it over."

"What did I steal? What are you talking about?"

"Jamal's bracelet. He had it when he went to bed last night, and now it's missing," she seethed.

"What?" I cried, my voice shaky. "Why do you think I stole it?"

"Don't act so surprised; I know you found it when you made his bed this morning, and you decided to keep it yourself," she said with cold assurance.

I should have known better than to question her, but the words blurted out of my mouth. "Does he remember going to bed with it?"

"Are you questioning me, you sneaky thief?"

I didn't know what possessed me to argue with her, but I said, "No, madam. He is still a child; he must have lost it at school."

She laughed and looked straight into my eyes. "Lost it? Are you saying he lost it in school? I can see how you have planned all the answers, but you can't outsmart me. You stole it and hid it somewhere in this house. I'll give you two hours to find it; one way or the other you are going to give it back to me," she commanded and left the room.

I knew it was going to be a long agonizing night for me. She really believed that I had stolen it. It was a heavy, thick bracelet, and I remembered seeing it on Jamal's hand and wondering why a child would be allowed to wear such expensive jewelry.

Helplessly, I waited in my room, praying and hoping that Jamal would find it before the end of those two hours. My prayers and wishes didn't do me any good. Lisha came back to my room exactly two hours later.

"Give it to me now!" she ordered. "This is your last chance."

"I didn't take it, madam. Please believe me," I pleaded.

"I'm going to take you to the police; they have a machine that can tell if you are lying, and then they will put you in jail."

What a great idea! my inner voice cried. "Take me to the police, madam, let them put me on the machine. I'm not a thief."

How lucky it would be if she took me to the police. That would be my escape! I could tell them what she was doing to me.

Lisha must have sensed my excitement; as if possessed by an evil spirit, she slapped me with both hands again and again until my face was burning, then pushed me to the floor, took the mop and hit me with it. Then she stomped on me, cursing and spitting as I moaned and curled up into a fetal position. I must have passed out before she left the room.

As if in a dream, I cried out in agony, *Amma, Amma!* When I came to I had a pounding headache and every inch of my body hurt. Covered with black and blue bruises, I dragged myself into the kitchen for vinegar to put on my head. I boiled some water and used a towel as a hot pack on my bumps, then applied oil to the bruises.

I lay in bed that night terrified. One day Lisha was going to kill me. No one would ever find out what happened to me, and all this suffering would be for nothing. Anger was searing inside me. How could I go on like this? When was it going to end?

"Where are you, God?" I prayed, my hands together. "Why can't you see my suffering? Why are all of these terrible things happening to me? What is the use of talking to you, Lord? I have nothing to thank you for. I have been faithful and believed in you always, but in return you give me grief; you have blessed me with suffering and made it worse each day. Haven't I been tested enough? What have I done to deserve such punishment? Through all my troubles and heartaches, I have never once turned away from you, but *you* have abandoned *me!* Who should I turn to now? *Is* there a God to hear my cries and see my sorrow—or will this be my last prayer to you? If you are there, God, show yourself to me; give me a sign! Give me proof to believe in you again! I challenge you, Lord, to show me a miracle! If you do not, today I will stop believing in you, no longer will I waste my time and words on blind faith. You are an illusion."

It was my last prayer to God, and I felt even worse. The agony made me ache for my mother, to curl up in her caring arms, to hear her loving voice and feel her tender touch on my bruised body, tending to me and taking care of me. I needed her as never before. The memories of her soothed me and comforted me that night, until I finally slept.

This time it took a longer to recover. My bruises were healing, the pain was lessening, but I had no spirit left in me to keep up the daily routine. On the worst days I took the chance of not completing certain chores and tricking Lisha into believing that I had done them.

A week went by without a big scene and the weekend came. The children were home and so was Lisha. I was on the balcony washing the floor when I saw a group of girls walking down below; it was the first time I'd seen anyone there. They looked up and saw me. If Lisha hadn't been home it would have been a good opportunity to throw my note to them or ask for their help.

To my surprise, one of the girls shouted at me in Sinhalese: "Hey, girl, don't stay in that house! That woman is crazy! Jump off the balcony and run away!"

Scared that Lisha would hear them, I pretended not to understand what they were saying. I couldn't even signal them to be quiet because Lisha would be watching me.

The girl shouted again, "She is going to kill you! Run away; jump off the balcony!"

Trying not to look at them, I continued washing the floor and cursed my luck for losing the only chance I had to ask for their help.

Once the girls were out of sight, Lisha called me into the kitchen.

"This is what you do when I'm not home—you talk to the people on the street. Do you know them?"

"No, madam."

"What were they saying?"

"I don't know, madam; I didn't understand."

"You think I believe you? You are a thief and a liar," she said, and hit my head with a pan. Then she twisted my ears. "Don't let me catch you talking with anyone!"

"Yes, madam," I said. She hit my face with a fist, and I lost my balance and fell to the floor.

"Get off the floor and get back to work without making a scene!" She kicked me and left the kitchen.

It was a good thing that Lisha couldn't control my mind. I began thinking about what the girl had said; she must be someone who knew Lisha and what she was capable of. All I knew was how I feared for my life; one of these days I was going to be killed. I had to find a way to escape from her.

Jump off the balcony. The thought came to me hesitantly at first, and I brushed it aside. Then it came back: *Jump off the balcony.* Not once, not twice, but repeatedly, until I was saying the words over and over again in my head and they started to sink in. Jump off the balcony. Was it possible to do that and survive? And if I survived, would I end up a cripple for the rest of my life? Or hit my head so hard that I went into a coma, or went crazy?

Eight weeks had gone by since I'd started working for Lisha. So far not a word had arrived from my parents, and I wondered if they were searching for me. They must have written to Mr. Zain, and he might have given the letters to Lisha. It was unlikely he would worry about me unless my parents started inquiring. I knew my parents would try to find me, but when they did, it would be too late.

Day and night I found myself hearing those words, *Jump off the balcony*. The more I thought about it, the clearer it became—that seemed to be the only way out. There was no other option. A little voice in my head asked, It is wrong to take your own life? Another voice said, No, I am not trying to take my own life, but trying to stay alive, taking a chance to survive. For days, for weeks, I fought with the voices in my head; sometimes I paced the balcony, looking down from each angle, wondering which would be the safest place to jump. Each time I looked down, chills ran through my spine.

As the days dragged on, the idea of jumping off the balcony seemed to settle in my mind. If I had the slightest chance of survival, it was better than being killed by Lisha. I didn't want to die, but if I did, I wanted my death to be of benefit to my son and my parents.

I knew I should take as many precautions as possible to survive the fall—jumping onto the concrete floor would be certain death. On the left side of the balcony, in front of the living room, the brick wall was too close to the building. That wouldn't be safe. Behind the kitchen was a clothesline that ran parallel to the railing; it would be impossible to jump from there. The safest place would be in front of Lisha's bedroom—there were small flowerbeds below, visible from the main entrance. I was counting on the guards there to find me as soon as I hit the ground.

After I had chosen the spot, it took me another couple of days to muster the courage. Guilt made me weak. I wrote two letters, one to my parents and the other to my son, explaining in both letters everything that had happened to me since I had come to Lebanon. I told them why I had to do this terrible thing. I begged my mother to watch over my baby and fight to get a settlement. The hardest part was asking my son's forgiveness for an action that would deprive him of the only real parent he had. Then I hid both letters between my clothes in the suitcase.

I felt better after writing to them. It was as though I was saying goodbye to my life. I was scared, mournful and angry, but also relieved. Finally, I was ready.

About five o'clock in the morning, dressed in my white uniform, I went out onto the balcony. It was still dark. The fading moon looked bleak in the sky. Behind the buildings the sky was lighting up. A blanket of silence lay over the neighborhood—not even birds singing; everything looked calm and peaceful. The whole town was still asleep. Holding on to the cold railing, I wondered, could this be my last moment in this world?

It had been fourteen weeks since I said goodbye to my son, and the memories of that day weakened my spirit. Tears poured down my cheeks. Choking with guilt, I questioned whether I was doing the right thing. Was this truly the only way? I waited for a response from my inner self—it didn't speak to me, and I didn't feel anything. I knew then that jumping was my only hope. For my son's sake and mine, I had to take this chance, not to die but to live.

Taking a deep breath, I filled my lungs with fresh air and felt the bitter cold wind on my skin. The floor was damp from the morning dew. Soon the sun would come out of hiding. I had to hurry. I tiptoed across the balcony until I stood in front of Lisha's room. The curtain covered the glass doors, so she couldn't see a thing even if she were awake. She would be up soon, I thought, and suddenly a great joy filled my heart, the joy of shocking her.

Energy surged through my body, I had no fear, only the joy of freedom, freedom from Lisha! With newfound courage, I stepped to the railing. Trying not to look down, I climbed over, turned around and, facing the balcony, held onto the cold iron with both hands. Placing my full weight on my right side, I let go with my left hand and foot. The promise I had made to God, never to pray to Him again, didn't seem to matter anymore; I still believed in Him and needed His forgiveness in case I died. So I closed my eyes and whispered, "If this is wrong, dear Lord, please forgive me!"

Then, with all the force I could summon, I jumped into the air.

PART II

A SRI LANKAN CHILDHOOD

Chapter 5

On the west coast of Sri Lanka, north of the capital city of Colombo, lies the fishing village of Negomboa, and there, nestled among the young coconut groves, was the house my family occupied when I was born. It was December 1956. My mother was sitting on the verandah watching a man gingerly navigate a tightrope from one coconut tree to another. He was collecting toddy, the juice of coconut flowers, making a tapping sound as he struck the coconut stem to extract the juice. Villagers love drinking this fresh white juice before it is turned into *arrack*, the traditional spirit of Sri Lanka.

It had been raining off and on all day and Amma decided to close the windows before the next downpour. Hauling herself out of the chair, she felt a cramp in her lower abdomen, followed by a jolt of back pain. A mother of four already, with an additional eight stepchildren, she recognized the sign with a sinking heart. She was eight months pregnant, and hadn't expected to deliver me for a few more weeks.

Amma staggered inside and, lowering herself onto a mattress of coconut husks, called out for help. My half-brother Aruna appeared in the doorway.

"Go and find the midwife!" she cried. "Hurry, there's not much time." Just then the sky split open with a great roar of thunder and lightning.

Aruna, who had just carefully combed his hair and put on his nice washed shirt, which he kept under his pillow to smooth the wrinkles, had no choice but to go out into the pouring rain. Hopping onto his rusty bicycle, he set out on the muddy road. Pebble-like raindrops struck his face and mud splashed his legs as he paddled furiously in search of the midwife.

No sooner had Aruna and the midwife slopped into my mother's room than I was born, claiming my rights as the thirteenth and youngest child. I must have sensed the disappointment in her eyes. Amma wanted a boy, and I commenced to cry my lungs out. But Amma sloughed off the disappointment and set about caring for me as best she could, considering her slim budget and huge brood.

She was about five feet tall, with long black hair down to her waist, an oval face and eyes that carried the shadow of her sorrows. Outdoors she wore a sari, which made her look like a schoolteacher, but at home she wore a kimono like a rich woman. Born to a rich and powerful father, a member of the district council who practically owned the town of Chilaw, Amma kept up the appearance of a high-class housewife even when we were almost starving to death.

That rich and powerful father died when Amma was a child, the family fell on hard times, and at the ripe age of five she was sent to live with her grandmother. My grandmother treated Amma like a servant and removed her from school after fifth grade. She ran away a couple of times and each time was hauled back. Eventually my grandmother forced her into marriage with her first cousin, a man Amma respected but didn't love. When he died seven years later, leaving her with three children, she protected them as she would her own eyes—refusing to subject them to the same fate of adoption that she had suffered.

Amma cast her net of love beyond just her offspring. A simple and kind-hearted woman who bore life's setbacks with patience, she believed in God, went to church regularly and helped anyone who came to her in need. No beggar was sent away empty-handed if Amma could help it.

My father was Manuel—Pappa to us kids. Pappa was a great man, powerful and mysterious. He too came from a wealthy family, and after being educated at an English school joined the seminary to become a Jesuit priest. He spoke Latin and fluent, educated English. One year before his ordination, disturbed by questions the church couldn't answer, he left the church and trained himself in the art of hypnosis and astral travel. Some say he walked through walls and floated on air. He was gifted with such tremendous intelligence that no one could argue with him or prove him wrong.

Each day Pappa took a swim in the sea and meditated on the beach at sunset. He was a strong swimmer—so strong, in fact, that he once swam all the way from Sri Lanka to India, or so the story went. As Pappa told it, one day while swimming in the ocean he dove down deep, seeing if he could reach the bottom. When he couldn't hold his breath any longer he resurfaced and tried to swim back to shore, but the current kept pulling him down. In grave danger, Pappa drew on his hypnotic powers, inducing a cataleptic state and suggesting to his subconscious that he would wake up only when land was within reach.

For several days he floated in the ocean, unconscious. A knocking sensation brought him to, his body being buffeted by waves. The coastline was within sight, but when he tried to swim back he discovered his arms were lying alongside his body, stiff as driftwood. To come out of the trance he resorted to rhythmic breathing, and presently his arms and legs loosened up and he set off for the shore. The huge waves sapped his energy, and exhausted from the struggle, he started yelling for help, whereupon a fisherman came to his rescue.

Pappa, as it turned out, had floated all the way to India, about two hundred and fifty miles away. This happened during World War II. No one believed his story and Indian officials, suspecting him of espionage, threw him into prison. After three months of questioning and cross-checking the references my father had given them, the government set him free and he was sent back to Sri Lanka. Pappa said it was his power of hypnotism that saved him in the water. All the Sri Lankan newspapers covered the story, and he became something of a legend.

People were awestruck by Pappa, and some were scared of him, thinking he was possessed by an evil spirit. When he walked down the street the seas would part as pedestrians stepped aside and bowed, taking off their hats. An aura of otherworldliness hovered about him. Even the family held him in awe. My mother once warned me, "Don't ever look straight into his eyes." Less inclined to superstition than the rest of my family, and more intrepid, I marched up to Pappa and gazed directly at him. Nothing happened.

Pappa loved all his children, but he was very strict with us. Woe to the child who failed a subject in school; the punishment was severe. My half-sister Neila was so scared of him she would wet her pants if he even talked to her. I was the only one who dared look straight at him, and the only one who got away with anything. I sat on his lap, listened to his stories and talked back to him.

Pappa was a handsome man who could charm any woman into his arms. When he met my mother he was a widower with eight children from two marriages. Though the prospect of such a large brood must have scared my mother, and though Sri Lankan culture frowned upon second and third marriages, she was unable to resist Pappa.

Following independence, the conservative government, the United Nation Party, was elected and stayed in power until 1956. To improve Sri Lanka's standard of living the government introduced and encouraged private enterprise. Pappa worked as an agent for an American insurance company and lived the good life. Like many good things, it came to an end. People say thirteen is an unlucky number; maybe having thirteen children between them brought bad luck to my parents. Soon after I was born a socialist government came to power in Sri Lanka and seized control of all private businesses. Pappa lost his job. He began practicing homeopathy without much success, and dabbling in hypnosis, and what was there to show for it? Pride—he was his own boss. How he supported his family of thirteen children was always a mystery to me.

My mother told me that when I was six months old, we had no food for several days and her breasts dried up. "In your sleep you started to moan and I tried to wake you, but you didn't open your eyes. Thinking you were dying, I ran to the kitchen, checked every empty rice bin and found a handful of crumbs to make porridge for you.

"The very next day, I took the bus to another town with Piumi and went begging from house to house. People gave us rice, potatoes, even some money. The last house was a big bungalow, and when the woman saw your sister she said, 'Have you no shame, woman? What are you doing roaming the streets with a young woman? Take her home and find another way to make a living.' I was so humiliated I never went begging on the streets again," Amma concluded, wiping her tears away.

Vaguely I remember my mother and half-sisters sitting in the living room packing tooth powder and rolling *beedi*, small cigars. Sometimes I would put the sticker around the beedi.

Like many people who fall on hard times, we moved from one residence to another. The houses we rented sat on land with lots of jacktrees nearby that produced five- to ten-pound fruit. Jackfruit, which when ripe turns yellow, juicy and sweet, can be sauteed as a curry, boiled or steamed, and eaten with coconut. Most of our meals would be jackfruit—stolen, since we weren't allowed to touch trees on rented land. Occasionally we had chicken, whenever a bird strayed over from a neighbor's house and my brothers nabbed it. That was a veritable feast, though with so many people in the house, each was entitled to just a small slab. Sometimes my brothers helped fishermen gather their nets and were rewarded with fish. But most days the cupboard was bare, and we would have to content ourselves with a piece of young coconut or a hot cup of tea. There were times I would walk into the kitchen and find my mother scraping the bottom of the black clay pan to get a handful of burnt rice. She would offer it to me, and not knowing it was her only share of food for the day, I would take it.

My playtime was spent under the trees, tinkering with old cans and coconut shells, waiting for fruit to fall—mangoes, guavas, olives—or for squirrels to drop their nuts. Berries in the bushes never escaped my eyes, and if I found a dead bird I brought the thing home hoping my mother would cook it.

Respect, in Sri Lanka, is earned through wealth, education, occupation, age, race, class and behavior. During all my parents' financial struggles Amma tried to keep up appearances, dressing us like rich children and cutting our hair short like Westerns'. Papa's title of doctor, his English education and the way he dressed; Western style had won him respect, but this was eroded by his having left the priesthood and married several times. These moves made him a social outcast among family and friends. Sri Lankans stubbornly adhered to the tradition of one marriage per person, no matter what the circumstances, and when my parents bucked that tradition, people talked behind their backs. Being ostracized didn't bother Pappa, but his bad reputation cast its shadow over us children.

One would think, as the youngest of thirteen, that I would have been lavished with attention, but that wasn't the case. Without toys I ran around the house like a little mouse, hiding in corners, witnessing the arguments between my half-siblings and my mother. They said Amma only cared for the children from her first marriage and mistreated her stepchildren. I didn't understand this. To me, we were all one family. I longed for their acceptance, and it hurt when they teased me. Once at a family gathering my half-sister Piumi asked my mother, "Why is Chuty-Nungi darker than us?"

"Don't you know?" one of my brothers said. "Pappa found her in the gutter covered with ants. He felt sorry for her and brought her home. She's not one of us."

Everyone laughed, but I didn't think it was funny. I ran into the yard and climbed an *araliya tree* (Temple Tree). Where are my real parents? Why did they throw me in the gutter? I wondered. A while later my sister Neila came looking for me. "Don't cry, Nungi, you are our sister, your brother's only teasing, don't believe him."

Neila's advice was lost on me. Invisible in my parents large brood, I was a self-pitying and jealous child—especially jealous of my sister Seetha, the only sibling born of the same two parents as I. Whenever we had visitors Seetha would hide behind the curtains and they would call out for her, oblivious to my attempts to capture their attention with smiles, songs and dances. Why do they want to see Seetha all the time? I would ask myself. Her beauty and innocence captivated everyone; I felt worthless, ugly and betrayed, and in revenge I used to lunge at her every chance I got, pinching her face and neck until my mother intervened and slapped my fingers, extracting a promise never to attack Seetha again. Craving love and fighting for attention, I ended up being the naughty girl, the wild child of the family. The only one who understood me, I thought, was my father—and Menica.

Most of my time was spent with Menica, who was only eleven years old when she came to live with us. My father brought her to our home from one of his trips to the hill country where her parents worked on a tea estate. Deceived by my father's wealthy appearance, Menica had begged him to bring her to our home. It was another mouth to feed, but my mother hadn't turned her away. Menica became the family servant.

She was dark, with a round muscular body and thick black hair tied up in a doughnut on her head. She played with me, fed me, bathed me and rocked me to sleep. When she worked, I climbed on her back and she never got mad at me.

"Menica, why is it no one loves me?" I asked her once.

"They love you, baby; they just don't have the time to show it," she said.

"Why did you come to live with us? Don't you miss your mother?"

"Your father looked so rich and powerful, I thought he could give me a better life. I also wanted to see the ocean. People up in the mountains talked about it all the time and said how beautiful it was and how it cries all day long. I wanted to see it with my own eyes."

"How could your mother let you leave her like that? Didn't she love you?"

"She loved me a lot, baby. She begged me to stay, but when I didn't listen she cursed me. She threw sand at me and said, 'You will never be happy in your life.'"

Shocked, I hugged her and said, "I love you, Menica. I promise to take care of you when I get older."

"Oh, baby, I love you too," she said.

"Why don't you go back to them?"

"Maybe one day I will…" she said, wiping away tears.

On my first day of school, I felt like a baby bird ready to soar. Dressed up in an old white uniform that had belonged to Seetha, I slipped my tiny feet into her old shoes and they fit perfectly. Amma took me by the hand and as we set off down the road several neighbors, who had been peeking through their windows, came out.

"Are you going to school, baby?" someone called.

I nodded and tried to keep up with Amma. Pulling on the curls that clustered around my neck, I walked carefully on the side of the road, trying to keep my shoes out of the sand.

It was a Catholic girl's school on the beach, surrounded by a six-foot brick wall, about a quarter of a mile from home. We went through the huge iron gate into the schoolyard and saw a group of children gathered under an *araliya tree*, which drooped with white, sweet-smelling flowers.

In the principal's office I placed my hands together as if I were going to pray. "God bless you, Mother," I said to the woman behind the desk.

"God bless you, Ranga," said the nun. She wore a white robe and black veil, which made her look like a penguin. "Welcome to our school." As my mother turned and left, the nun took my hand and walked me over to a class full of children. My teacher was Mother Jones, a kindly woman who showed me to my desk and chair. I felt so grown up having my own desk and chair.

The school building was one huge hall divided into many classes, from grade one to grade twelve, and I could hear the voices of the other teachers. Amazingly, the students sat quietly at their desks and spoke only when addressed.

During lunch break we stood in a line while the older students served us milk and sweet buns. The milk tasted sweet and warm in my mouth; I wondered if I could ask for a second. At the sound of the principal's bell the children would form lines in the yard and file back to class, slowly and quietly. Mother Teresa, long cane in hand, watched with an eagle eye. Anyone who misbehaved was caned then and there.

At the end of my first day we were sent into the yard to wait for our parents. All the other children left with their parents, but my mother was nowhere to be seen. I didn't know what to do or where to go. Mother Jones saw me and came to my rescue.

"Don't be sad, child. I'll take you to your sister and she'll escort you home."

Seetha was in the second grade at the time and had to stay for two more periods. The teacher let me sit next to her until school was over. Mortified, I began crying.

Seetha whispered in my ear: "Please don't cry, Nango," which meant little sister. "You're embarrassing me. I'll take you home soon." I was tired and fell asleep at the desk. After that I learned to walk back home by myself.

I thrived in school and did well in my studies. My ability to sing and dance made me a star on the school stage, but it didn't impress my parents.

"Girls are expected to behave more modestly. Dancing on stages is not for good girls," said Amma.

Once a film producer saw a performance of mine and asked me to play a part in a film. Pappa crushed my hopes. "I don't want my daughter to be an actress; it isn't respectable."

How respectable was it to be moving from house to house? We were an itinerant family, evicted from one home after another for not paying the rent on time, moving from town to town. At least the houses were large, with brick walls, cement floors and good-sized gardens.

My favorite house was one in Kapungoda, within walking distance of the beach and closer to my new school. An old couple lived in a mansion nearby; the husband was a fiscal officer in the village. Amma didn't usually allow us to visit our neighbors or have close friendships with them—she wouldn't risk losing our cover as a rich family—but somehow we started spending a lot of time with this couple. Aunty and Uncle Fiscal had no children and loved us all dearly, especially Seetha, whom they wanted to adopt.

Their yard was covered with all kinds of flowers and vegetables and had a nice landscaped area where all the children in the neighborhood came to play. Aunty and Uncle Fiscal always had enough food to feed the whole village. At lunch and dinnertime their table would be laden with platters of fish, meat and produce. Often we ate there. What a pleasure it was not having to fight for the bigger piece of fish or chicken. Sometimes when they had visitors, Menica would help Aunt Fiscal with the cooking. In return, she came home with leftovers that would feed us for a couple of days.

It was in Kapungoda that I had my first communion, at the age of seven. I had expected it to be as joyful as my sister Seetha's. Amma dressed me up in a new white uniform and placed a crown of fresh jasmine on my head.

"Why can't I have a nice dress like the one you made for sister at her communion?" I said.

"We're not Catholic anymore. I'm just letting you do this because you're in a Catholic school."

"If we're not Catholic, what are we?"

"We've converted to Seventh Day Adventist, and I can't come to the service with you."

"It's wrong to go to a different church, Amma," I said, disappointed.

"Once you start going to the Adventist church, you'll see the difference."

And so I went to my first communion with Menica. All the other girls looked pretty and happy in their shiny silk gowns with their families clustered around them. As I walked down the aisle to the altar in my makeshift dress, I felt like a homeless child. I kept turning back to see if Amma had changed her mind and come. After the service I went back to the school for the reception, determined to hate my mother forever. When I returned home Amma took me to a studio to have my picture taken, hoping that would cheer me up, but nothing could replace the emptiness inside.

At the end of that school year my parents introduced me to the Adventist church and enrolled me in its private school. Just as Amma had predicted, I enjoyed that church and gained a better understanding of God. My schoolteacher was Miss Isabel. Miss Isabel, who would stop to help an animal cross the road and made a point of not stepping on ants, said she had visions of Jesus and heard his voice. Her stories inspired me and I tried to be like her, an honest Christian. It was a comfort to hear that God loved me when I felt no one else did, and I prayed and prayed, imploring Him to show His love for me. I saw Jesus in my dreams and became a strong believer.

A year later Pappa decided to send all us children to the Adventist boarding school up in the mountains, a couple of hundred miles away. It was an American school run by the Adventist mission and most of the classes were in English. Since he couldn't afford to pay the full tuition, the church offered us a work-study program.

At the age of eight, I was too young to be away from home; I missed my mother and cried each time she visited us. During the summer holidays Amma decided to keep Seetha and me home. My other siblings returned to the school in the mountains. Some found future husbands or wives there and were married with the parents blessings, while others had a chance to enter foreign schools to further their education.

Seetha and I went back to the Catholic school, where it was a struggle to be Adventists. Not allowed to go to school activities on Saturday, which was the Adventist holy day, we often missed a class or an exam or a concert, and weekend sports were out of the question. Nor did I take the religion class. During that period I sat at the back of the class and did my own work. Sometimes I couldn't help listening to the priest who was teaching the class. If he said anything that I believed contradicted the Bible, I questioned him. The principal and the teachers didn't like my outspokenness, but as an Adventist, my knowledge of the

Bible was now far beyond that of my peers. So was my knowledge of English, after a year at the American school. I was the first in my class every year, and the teachers had no grounds for complaint.

Chapter 6

We were moving again, this time to our own place close to my mother's hometown of Chilaw, a coastal fishing village thirty miles north of Negombo. Under Sri Lanka's new socialist government, Amma had found a way to claim land being distributed to the villages.

I sat in the moving van between the driver and my father as we passed through Chilaw and continued down a gravel road where there were two Hindu temples with statues that towered above the dusty landscape—many-handed Vishnu, Kali Amma with her bloody tongue, Ghana the elephant head. Beyond the temples it was as if we were entering another world: as far as the eye could see, lily-choked lakes and acres of partly wooded, parched land. The dust-coated shrubs along the road appeared lifeless and irritable for not being able to show their true colors. Despite the presence of lakes it seemed as if rain had never touched this part of the earth.

Farther along we came across rice paddies. The long grass-like plants, having reached their full height of some two feet, were flopped over in a tangle and waving in the wind, rubbing against one another with a hissing sound. Then there was a tree with a huge trunk whose rope-like roots hung from the branches down to the ground. On the trunk, about three feet from the ground, was a hollow space filled with flowers, fruit and something that was smoking. My father said it was a *Nuga* tree (Banyan), and that the *Hindu* villagers worshiped it.

"You can see our house from here!" cried Amma.

Expecting a huge brick house like the ones we had rented, I made out a roof made of coconut leaves and a small wooden shack. The moving truck pulled up and I climbed out. This was our new home—one room divided in half by a screen of sacks. The floor was cement-mixed sand, rough to the touch. Toward the back a door led to a small kitchen. There was no toilet, just an outhouse. I'll never be able to bring my friends home, I thought, my heart sinking. The family was small now that the older children had moved away, only Seetha, my half-sister Milred and myself. Still, it seemed much too small for five people.

Outside, a narrow path led to a well filled with muddy water that looked like milk tea. A stone's throw away was a little pond surrounded by sugarcane and covered with *Kohila,* a thorny water plant. I searched for other houses in the area and, not seeing any at first, got the impression that we were alone.

The field behind the house was calling out to me and I ran to it, mesmerized by the huge empty sky all around me. It seemed as if I were standing in the center of the universe. Far away on the horizon a border of woodlands scraped the sky. It was utterly quiet save for the whispering wind and the sighing paddy fields, gossiping birds and creaking insects.

I wandered into the field and spied another house at the edge of our property. So we weren't all alone. It was bigger than ours, with a roof of coconut leaves and walls of clay. Clotheslines crisscrossed the yard and someone had spread clothing all over the grass to dry. It must belong to *dhobies*, I thought, going up to the fence. Dhobies were traditional washer folk. A girl who seemed my age popped out of the house and smiled. "We just moved here. My name's Ranga," I called out.

"I'm Indra," she said, and quickly retreated inside. Maybe she's shy, I thought, excited nonetheless to have found a friend. In the days to come, Indra would smile at me whenever she crossed our land to get to the street, but her family's low caste as *dhobies* prohibited us from pursuing a closer relationship.

Returning to the gravel road I discovered yet another house on the other side and a few more farther along. Though the set-up was disappointingly rustic, life at the farmhouse soon became an adventure. In the village I talked with everyone and tried to befriend them, despite my mother's disapproval.

"I wish you were a boy, but you came into this world as a girl so you need to act like one, my dear child," said Amma when she saw me waving to a group of children on the road. "Stop running around, talking and laughing at everyone you see. Stop acting like a boy. Girls are supposed to be gentle, soft-spoken and shy. Look at your sister and learn from her."

"I could never be better than Seetha," I muttered and stomped off.

Amma worked hard in the fields, growing vegetables and planting coconut in the dry, cracked clay. Close to the house she grew papaya, banana, mangoes and lime, built a hen house and kept a cow for milk. The land farther off was reserved for a paddy field. It was a hard life, but it gave my mother peace of mind. She didn't have to worry about paying the rent anymore or counting the days until she would be able to buy more food—the vegetables, fruit and rice from our land filled our stomachs. We had plenty to eat and even made money selling the extra produce to traders on their way to market.

My father, like a bird without wings, lay in his armchair reading books while my mother did all the hard work out in the fields and in the house. He had a bicycle to get to the main road, where he caught a bus to his private clinic in town. It was Milred, the youngest of three from my mother's first marriage, who helped Amma with the housework while Seetha and I stayed buried in our books.

There were only a few drinking wells in the village. The one closest to us was about half a mile away. My mother sent Milred or me to fetch the water. We made at least two trips a day to the well, using clay pots, which I tried to carry on my hip or my head as the villagers did, without success. It was hard work, and I often wondered why Amma never sent Seetha to the well.

Pappa said it was healthy to take a shower before sunrise. In the dry season, taking a shower at the family well was no better than rinsing our bodies with dirt. We would apply soap to our hair and after rinsing it off, pour on lime juice to kill the salt. On weekends we walked to a nearby lake for a bath.

We had to be cautious in the fields, which were crawling with cobras, pythons and other poisonous snakes. Sometimes we found them inside our house and on the roof between the coconut leaves. Frightened by reports of deaths in the village from snakebites, Amma would check our beds and every corner of the house before we retired for the night. She became an expert snake killer.

Late one night I awoke to the sound of footsteps right outside our room. I thought it was Amma going into the shack. Then I heard her voice, "Who is that?" and footsteps running away. I jumped off the bed; Seetha woke up and whispered, "Don't make a noise!" We glanced at the open window, thinking the thief might come slipping through. Paralyzed with fear, I sat back down and wet the bed.

"Keep your eyes on the window and I'll pray," Seetha whispered, kneeling down.

After a while Amma came inside and I heard her say to Pappa, "I saw him; he was going to steal the cow. I ran after him but he got away." When she popped her head into our room to make sure we were all right, she was out of breath and still holding the heavy rod that she kept beside her bed. After that night I slept with the Bible under my pillow, believing it would protect me from evil.

Early in the morning, through the mist, the gravel road came to life with schoolchildren. In their white uniforms and white tennis shoes they looked like swans in a brown pond. My sister and I went to a Catholic convent in Chilaw, close to the bus stand. Mornings were cool enough, but by the time school let out the sun would be beating down on the dusty gravel road and our uniforms stuck to our skin and sweat rolled down our bodies. We used umbrellas to block the sun. I wrapped my books with plastic to keep the sweat off. When we reached the *Nuga* tree by the side of the road we would rest in the shade and swing on the long hanging roots with the other kids. The family that lived close by placed a big clay pot of water with a coconut shell there to quench our thirst.

Rainy season brought relief from the dust. The heavy drops would hit the roof with a rhythmic sound, inducing the desire to sleep in on school mornings. The first year we lived on the farm I wandered into the kitchen, embraced by the cool, fresh air, wondering how we would get to school through the flooded village. The wood stove was burning, its yellow flames caressing the black kettle. I perched on a stool beside the fire to sip my morning tea, which Amma had made with rainwater. She had also heated some water for us to wash up.

"Amma," I said, "how are we going to go to school?"

"The roads are all right," she assured me. "You have to walk barefoot and carry your shoes to the main road. There's a house just before the bus stop where you can wash your feet and put your shoes back on."

Indeed, glancing out the window I saw the other children gingerly wading down the road with their shoes in hand. So we had no choice but to get ready and join them.

Gripping my books under my arm, umbrella in one hand and white tennis shoes in the other, I stepped into the water, which was about a foot deep. Rain had washed away the gravel and the clay had turned into slippery mud. Villagers who had never worn shoes in their life had no trouble navigating through the slop, and one woman told me, "Step with your toes, not your heels, and try to press your big toe down hard in the mud. That will keep you from slipping."

With only two uniforms to wear to school, and one then at the *dhobies'* house, I was afraid of falling. As for Seetha, she was boiling mad, her face so red I could have burned mustard seed on it. Seetha hated village life. Every day she blamed Amma for bringing us there. "If I ever get a chance to leave this place," she vowed, "I'll never come back!" Still jealous, I hoped her dream would come true.

Evening just before sunset, I sat under the cherry tree that Amma had planted in the front yard and let my imagination flow. The clouds turned yellow, orange and red, as if heaven had opened its doors, and the sun would float like a huge red balloon toward the horizon. It gave me a profound sense of peace to behold this sight, and with the few notes my brother Milroy had taught me I would strum the guitar, singing my favorite song:

> I am nobody's child, I am nobody's child,
> Just like a flower, I am growing wild,
> No Mummy's kisses, and no daddy's smile
> Nobody wants me; I am nobody's child.

Some evenings under the cherry tree I would try to capture nature's beauty on a piece of paper, drawing and composing verse. Overcome by joy, I would call Pappa to share the experience. He always joined me, praising my drawings and listening to my poems. If I called Amma she would just say, "Go inside and study, don't waste your time." I was thinking of becoming a doctor, and Amma wanted to keep me on track.

But she couldn't take away my joy in nature. The breeze spoke to me, opening my mind to new paths and ideas. I spent hours in the field watching the sky, listening to the insects, gazing at the woods, wishing a fairy would find me or that I could disappear there and live with the animals the way Tarzan had.

Saturday was Amma's day off. That day she didn't have to cook or clean. We went to church as a family and afterwards visited patients in the hospital.

One Saturday, after I had just turned ten, I put on a special dress. Seetha and I had rehearsed a hymn to sing in church, and I hoped everyone would notice me in my dress. I wanted to look as pretty as my sister—to hear someone say, just once, that I was beautiful.

At the end of the service, a boy I hadn't noticed before came and stood in front of me.

"That was very nice. You have a beautiful voice," he said. Surprised, and overcome by shyness—which wasn't like me—I forgot my manners and ran away from him. The following Saturday his eyes followed me everywhere, and though I soaked up the attention, to which I wasn't accustomed, at the same time it made me nervous. Whenever he tried to speak to me I ran away, afraid my parents would notice.

His name, I found out, was Geoffrey. He was a Burgher boy, one of the racially mixed children of Portuguese or Dutch fathers and Sinhalese mothers. Though citizens of Sri Lanka, they looked, acted and dressed like Europeans, and English was their mother tongue. Geoffrey wasn't particularly handsome, but I was attracted to his charming smile and innocent expression. He was skinny, tall, and combed his shiny black hair to the side. He spoke gently and politely to everyone, and with great respect.

I began counting the days until Saturdays. In church Geoffrey and I started exchanging glances and sneaking quick smiles. It gave me chills whenever our eyes met.
One day when he handed me the hymnal, I found a small note inside. I hid it in my bra and ran to the bathroom. There were three questions written in English:

What is your full name?
When and where were you born?
Are you really in love with me (Yes/No)?

Laughing, I reveled in the strange new feeling that ran through my body and made my knees weak.

Though I wanted to reply right away, I wasn't sure of my English writing skills and didn't want him to know my weakness. I could read and understand English fine, but that was the extent of my knowledge. And so I took the note to Shelly, a friend whom I thought could be trusted with my secret. She helped me answer his note. I begged her and Geoffrey both to keep it a secret from my family and the church members. After that day Geoffrey and I exchanged letters through the church hymnal. He wrote to me in English, and Shelly helped me answer him in English. After a while I got tired of English and started to answer him in Sinhalese.

It would have been heartbreaking news to my family if they ever found out that I had a boyfriend, especially at the age of ten. I could destroy my character by getting involved with a male without my parents' approval. As a Sri Lankan girl, I wasn't allowed to have social relationships with men other than my relatives or family friends. If I did make the mistake of becoming involved with someone, there would be no room for change of heart—I would eventually have to marry the object of my affection, or else be despised by neighbors, an irreversible curse. Gossip could destroy a woman's character. No amount of good behavior afterward could erase the scars of indiscretion. Indeed, parents went to great lengths to protect their daughters from wagging tongues—grounding them, beating them and getting them into early marriages.

Needless to say, I was afraid of becoming embroiled in romance—and the fear was matched by my elation.

Who needed to talk? Through letters alone, I fell in love with Geoffrey—as much in love as a ten-year-old can be. For the first time in my life I was happy and nothing else seemed to matter. This wasn't your average puppy love, over in a matter of weeks. The months kept passing and the letters kept coming. Geoffrey filled an emptiness inside me, and I sensed his presence everywhere I went.

Church was now my favorite place to be—I didn't miss a single prayer meeting or youth gathering. One glimpse of my love at church was food to my soul. Whenever he went up to the pulpit with the pastor I locked eyes with him, which filled me with an achy sweet joy.

Like a good Sri Lankan girl, I didn't desire physical contact. The fact that he loved me was satisfaction enough.

I was twelve when I came of age. It happened in school, at lunch break.

"Ranga, there is a stain on the back of your uniform," said Letitia. Letitia was the only friend I had in school. Nobody else liked to hang around with her because of her crossed eyes and hunchback, but I did because she was an accomplished artist and wrote beautiful poems.

I twisted around and in horror beheld the bloody splotch on the back of my white uniform. I made a mad dash for the toilet and pulled down my underwear. Why I was bleeding? Letitia was standing on the other side of the door.

"There's something wrong with me, Letitia—I'm bleeding," I said, cracking the door.

She gave me an inquisitive look. " Are you a *big girl*?"

Suddenly I remembered the lesson in biology class, about how every girl comes of age.

"Is this your first time?" Letitia pressed.

"Yes," I said. "What do I do now?"

"Oh Ranga, I have to tell the principal. She'll inform your parents. Don't come out, stay in there; I'll be right back." She ran off to the principal's office while I closed the door and waited.

With sudden joy, I thought, I'm a *big girl*! Ever since that lesson in biology class, I had wanted to be one.

Now my family would pay more attention to me. I would wear a real bra so my large breasts wouldn't bounce and I would read novels, go to movies and do all the other things big girls did.

A few minutes later, Sister Gabriel came and knocked on the toilet door. "You can come out now, Ranga. I've sent a message to your parents. I don't know how they want us to handle this. Until they get here you have to stay in the girl's hostel. Now keep your face down and follow me."

Awkwardly, I followed her to the hostel. She sent me into a room, put some old newspapers on a chair and asked me to sit on it. "Take it easy and wait here until your mother arrives," she said and left the room.

So I waited and waited. By the time Amma appeared in the room, it was late afternoon. School was over, and it was quiet. She took a white bed sheet out of her bag. "I have to cover you before I take you outside," she said. " It's bad luck to see men at this time." She put the bed sheet over my head, covering my face. "Don't look at anyone—don't peek," she ordered, guiding me out of the hostel and into a taxi.

Curious as always, I peeked through the sheet and spotted the male driver, a skinny young fellow, then quickly buried myself again, fearing what bad luck would do to me.

Coming of age was an occasion to be celebrated in Sri Lanka. Since I was the last one in the family and almost all of my brothers and sisters were married and gone, Amma decided to throw a party and invite all the family. My half-brothers and -sisters from my father's side had distanced themselves from the family. They visited Pappa at Christmas but didn't speak to Amma. In spite of the tension my mother decided to invite everyone to the celebration.

Following Sinhalese tradition, Amma went to a Buddhist monk and got my horoscope. According to the stars I was to stay indoors for three days and not wash my hair. Afterwards I had to shower with herb water at a certain time and wear a white dress. Those were three of the longest, loneliest days of my life. I spent them imprisoned in my tiny room, counting the hours until I emerged like a butterfly from her cocoon—a big girl.

At the end of my sentence, Amma covered me head to toe again with a white sheet, led me out of the room to a small water tank that was filled with flowers, leaves and special kinds of fruit. She asked me to close my eyes as she removed the sheet and poured seven pots of water over my head. Then I was allowed to take a full shower. She gave me a mixture of raw egg and herbal oil drink, which I had a hard time swallowing. After I was dressed in a white gown that Amma had made, she guided me into the living room and asked me to open my eyes.

The table was laden with jewelry, money and flowers, as well as traditional Sinhalese dishes, among them *caum, cokkis* (oil cakes), bananas and *kiribath,* rice made with milk to indicate a new beginning.

"Take a good look at the table. Your life should be filled with all these. You are a grownup now, and you can't behave like a child anymore," Amma said, hugging me. Pappa came over and squeezed me hard. His shaved beard brushed my cheeks as he kissed me and placed more money in my hand. "Buy anything you want with this money," he said.

I came out of the house and looked around. Nothing had changed. The dusty road, the dry fields and the warm air felt the same. One by one my relatives arrived, sisters, brothers, close aunts and uncles, all bearing gifts. I received new dresses, perfume, books, pens and money, but none of that was as thrilling as having my big family all around me.

Pappa looked so proud and happy to be with his children. My half-sisters Neila and Malie started to talk with Amma again, and that made me the happiest of all. Amma had cooked for the whole family; it was a feast of joy. We danced and sang through the night.

I received a gift from Geoffrey at church the next Saturday, a bottle of perfume. Embarrassed, I avoided eye contact with him.

Now that I was a grownup, I felt pressure to act my age. I had to be more careful about Geoffrey. People were watching me, waiting with their sharp tongues and prying eyes to spin stories.

We continued our relationship through letters and managed to keep it from our parents for three years. At the end of the third year, Mrs. Berg, Geoffrey's mother, gave me a mean look at church. Later I saw her talking with Amma. I knew it was trouble, and I was frightened. Geoffrey gave me a note saying that his mother had found out about us and was going to tell my parents. He promised that nothing they did would change his feelings about me and that he was going to talk to my father. "Please don't; that's not a good idea," would have been my response, but I had no way of telling him that.

By the time I reached home, I was sick from fright and started throwing up. My parents had to stay behind for a meeting and when they finally came home it was close to sunset. Amma's eyes were burning with anger. "What is all this talk about you having an affair with Geoffrey? Is it true?"

I sat there, mute.

"You're still a child. I can still smell the milk on your breath. What is your hurry to find a man?"

Pappa called me into the front room, where he was sitting at his medicine table.

"Tell me honestly, what is it you want to do?" he asked. "Do you want to continue your education and be a doctor, or do you want to quit school and get married?"

Marriage had never crossed my mind, and I was embarrassed to hear him talk about it. At the same time I was mad, mad at him for asking, and my stubborn instinct made me want to yell, *Yes, I want to get married, and leave this house!* But I knew enough not to insult Pappa, so I kept quiet.

He took my hand, dragged me out to the front yard, broke a small branch from the guava tree and started to whip my bare backside. Pappa had doled out physical punishments to some of my siblings, but he had never struck me in my life. The thin guava cane slashed into my bottom and it started to burn. I tried to shield myself with my hand but he kept on whipping me, over and over again. I wanted to run away from him but that would have just made things worse. Finally he stopped and said, "Are you going to put an end to this?"

I yelled, "Yes," but inside I was more determined than ever. I would never stop loving Geoffrey, I told myself.

"If you want to go to school, you have to put this love business aside. You need your full attention on your education. You have to promise me never to write to him again, or even to look at him. If I get any news about the two of you ever again, I'm going to remove you from school and marry you off to someone."

Amma, who had watched me being whipped, hadn't tried to stop him. I hated her for that. Retreating to my room, I flopped down on the bed and burst into tears while she came to me with a bottle of oil, pulled my pants down and started to wipe my sores.

"You're still a baby; you have many long years before you need a man in your life. You must put your education first. Education is the key to everything. It can buy you everything, anything you want in life, and without it you are worth nothing. I don't want you to suffer the way I did. I want my children to have a better life. You can get married to a rich man and have a good life. If you don't behave well now, these things are going to reflect poorly on your character."

She was going on and on like a broken record. I wanted to scream, *Nothing you say can stop me from loving him!* But not wanting another beating, I held my tongue.

My parents must have thought it would teach me a lesson; instead, it reinforced my love.

The next day when Amma went to the store, I was sitting under the cherry tree working on a poem. I must have inherited my father's psychic ability because suddenly I sensed Geoffrey's presence. Far down the road a figure was approaching on a bicycle. With gathering alarm, I watched as it grew larger and larger and presently morphed into the familiar figure of my love. Pappa was home. Mingled with my fear was shame—shame over my family's poverty.

After gathering up my papers, I dashed into the kitchen and hid there. By and by there was a knock on the door. Pappa answered. "Geoffrey? So, you got my message?"

"Yes, sir, I came as soon as I could."

"Please come on in; have a seat."

"I need to talk to you about Ranga," said Geoffrey.

Trembling in my hiding place, I could hear every word clearly.

"That's the reason I called you here," Pappa said. "What's going on between the two of you?"

" Please don't mind my mother; I know she has spoken to you. Listen to what I have to say about this matter." He paused. "You are different from other people, and I respect you, sir. I came to ask for your permission to love your daughter. I love her very much and promise never to hurt her or destroy her good name. After she has completed her education, when we are both old enough, I promise to marry her. I am willing to wait as long as it takes. Please don't hurt her; give us your permission and that will take the weight off her mind. She will pay more attention to her studies. I want her to study hard and become a doctor just as she wanted, and I'll be a pastor. Please don't pressure her to end this now. Give us your approval to love each other. That's all I ask of you, sir."

What a speech! I wanted to kneel down and kiss his feet, tell him how much I loved him. Patiently I waited to hear my father's answer.

"You should never make a promise you can't keep," Pappa said. "You're a fine young man, Geoffrey. I've always liked you, but my daughter is very precious to me. I can't let anyone hurt her. You're both too young to understand about love and keeping promises. Your parents want this stopped right now. You must understand, it's terribly difficult for me to hear someone say that my daughter is not good enough for her son. I cannot tolerate that disrespect."

"Please forgive me for my parents; that's why I came to you, sir, to assure you about my feelings toward her. I'm not going to stop loving her, but I don't want her punished. My parents can punish me all they want; I can take it as long as Ranga is safe."

"You're an honest man, and I have to respect that, but you need to think hard before you make any promises to my daughter. I will not encourage this, but I promise not to punish her. She has to complete her education, and in the meantime you can write to each other, and that's all. I trust you to keep your word and not to do anything that will destroy her reputation."

"Thank you, sir," Geoffrey said. With that, he walked out the door, hopped on his bicycle and paddled down the gravel road. I snuck out to the banana trees and watched him disappear into the woods.

Pappa never said anything about Geoffrey to me again. A strong believer in promises, he took Geoffrey's word seriously and regarded his request as a proposal to marry me. My parents' approval gave me the freedom to continue our communication through letters without creating a scandal.

Geoffrey was proud of himself for facing up to my father. In his next letter he asked me to study harder to reach our goal. He said he wanted to be a pastor, and had to go to India to get his degree, but he wouldn't leave the country until I completed the twelfth grade. He promised to wait, hoping that I would accompany him as he pursued his higher studies. I am important, he loves me, I thought. My life was complete! I started to pay more attention to school; I wanted to study hard and make him proud of me. My world began to grow, fed by hopes and dreams.

In the meantime he suffered his family's disappointment. His family disapproved of our relationship because of my parents' bad reputation and also because I wasn't part white and didn't speak English. His mother was furious with him for delaying his higher studies. She did everything in her power to break us apart. When all her attempts failed, she managed to get him out of town. Geoffrey was sent away to the Adventist school up in the mountains to work as a teacher.

Before leaving, he wrote me a letter promising to marry me and to love me for the rest of his life, and signed it with his blood. What depth of commitment! I thought, convinced that the separation would bring us even closer together.

Soft whispers and the smell of smoke from the wood stove woke me up. Patting the other side of the bed, I realized that Seetha was already up.

At last, the day I had been waiting for was finally here—Seetha was leaving home for good, going to Pakistan to become a nurse. All night long I had been dreaming about how she had missed the train and was coming back home.

The twin bed I had shared with Seetha for many years, our bodies arranged in opposite directions, would be mine now. I felt her pillow with my feet, kicked it to the floor and moved to the center of the bed. The birds had begun their dawn twittering in praise of the creator. A rooster crowed in the backyard, followed by others throughout the village—the first wake-up call of the day. Outside it was still dark. The kerosene lamp that had been burning all night long was still alive, the flame dancing in the breeze from the open window. Retrieving my mother's soft nylon sari, bunched at the foot of the bed, between cold toes, I covered myself, feeling nice and warm again.

The familiar click, click from the kitchen was my mother whisking egg with sugar before pouring hot coffee over it, Pappa's favorite breakfast. He was at the well taking his morning shower. Every few seconds the sound of splashing water made me shiver.

Over the years, nothing had changed between Seetha and me. She never did anything wrong; her behavior, her character, her beauty were praised by all. With her soft, fair skin, long eyelashes and red lips, her hair falling in gentle ringlets to her shoulders, my sister truly did look like an angel. Unlike me, she was shy. She spoke quietly and walked gracefully. She was the star in the family, and I still hadn't conquered my jealousy.

Now that she was leaving home it would be joy for me, life without competition.

Seetha rolled out of bed and began brushing her hair in front of the mirror. She made soft squeaky noises and wiped her eyes on her nightgown. I could see her in the mirror, her face puffy and red from crying. Suddenly she whirled around and gazed at me, and I shut my eyes.

"Nungo, are you awake?" she whispered in the darkness. *Nungi* is the Sinhalese word for younger sister, but Seetha changed it to Nungo, a special nickname. Every time she called me Nungo, it almost melted my cold heart.

"I left you all my nice clothes, but please give a couple of dresses to Milred," she said.

This is getting better and better! I thought. Not only will I have the twin bed to myself, I'll have all her clothes, too. Maybe I should open my eyes and kiss her goodbye; then again, it's better that I pretend to be asleep. I lay there unable to make up my mind and heard her walking toward me.

She sat down on the bed, her warm hand resting on my shoulder, shaking me gently. Her face was close to my ears and she smelled of jasmine soap. She whispered my name again. "Nungo? Nungo?" I didn't move. She waited a second, then spoke again. "I have to leave now, Nungo." Her voice was breaking up. Her cold wet lips brushed my cheeks. "Goodbye, Nungo; I love you very much. No matter what you think of me, I love you. Don't ever forget that."

Then she got up and left the room. I lay there stiff as a log, fighting back my own tears. I didn't hate her! All I felt now was sadness and an urge to run after her. She was still in the living room, weeping softly as she said goodbye to my parents.

My father had been praying, asking God to protect her on her journey and through all the years that she would be living away from home.

"Do you have everything? Where is the passport?" he said now.

"Don't worry, Pappa; I didn't forget anything. My passport is in my purse."

"All right, let's go then. We can't miss the train."

Hearing their footsteps fading and the front door closing, I opened my eyes. The flame on the kerosene lamp had died, along with my struggle. Darkness was fading, light sneaking through the wooden walls. Soon the sun would rise and in a few seconds my sister would be gone. Suddenly I sprang out of the bed, stumbled over the pillow I had kicked off earlier, and falling, hit my head on the edge of the bed. "Ouch!" But there was no time to feel sorry for myself. Gathering myself up from the floor, I rubbed my head and scurried out of the house into the front yard.

The smell of roses and gardenias filled the cool air. Pappa was climbing onto the bullcart, Seetha right behind him. Hurry! a voice inside me cried. My bare feet sinking into the sand, I swiftly tiptoed onto the narrow grass-filled pathway and then broke into a run, but by the time I reached the road it was too late—the cart was already well on its way, transporting Seetha farther and farther from me. Bells on the bull's neck jingled and the cartwheels made a cracking noise as they rolled over the gravel.

That morning, for the first time in thirteen years, I realized that I loved my sister. She was too far away to see me but I waved at her anyway, and kept waving, with tears rolling down my cheeks and a cold breeze blowing through the ragged holes in my nightgown. My feet were wet from the morning dew. Hugging myself to stave off the chill, I stood there watching the cart until it disappeared under the huge *Nuga* tree.

"Come inside before you catch cold," Amma said, walking back to the house.

The bright red sun was just peeking over the horizon, illuminating the clouds with its magnificent glow, and the mist was slowly disappearing from the lonely, empty road. How could I tell Seetha how sorry I was for hurting her, for scarring her lovely face with my fingernails? Burdened by guilt, I plunked down under my favorite cherry tree and cried. There was no need to hide my tears anymore. Seetha couldn't see me.

Amma called again. "Come inside and have your tea before it gets cold."

Wiping my eyes and nose on my nightgown, I ran inside the house and made up my mind to write a letter asking Seetha's forgiveness for hurting her and for not saying goodbye, and that was just what I did.

Not knowing the meaning of the saying, Be careful what you wish for, you might just get it, I had wished to get my sister out of my life, and now that she was, I began to miss her. That feeling of longing intensified when Sri Lanka entered a reign of terror.

I woke up to the sound of fireworks. The sun hadn't risen yet and my parents had been huddled around the radio all night, listening to the election results. The disappointment in Pappa's voice told me that his United Nation Party had lost. UNP, which had lost the elections in 1956 and 1960, had returned to power in 1965. Now, in 1970, the socialist Sri Lanka Freedom Party had overturned the conservative UNP government.

Though I felt bad for my father, I didn't understand why it mattered who won the election. Sri Lankans, who often fought over meaningless things, always celebrated their election victories violently, no matter who won. After an election every household that supported the winning party would celebrate by shooting fireworks. Life was not as good for the supporters of the losing party. They would have to go into hiding or else risk physical assault. The post-election period was a time for setting fire to houses, crops and businesses, and beating people. The violence would continue for a week, then die down.

Once the celebration was over in 1970, people began to digest what it meant for Sri Lanka. The new Freedom Party introduced the Land Reform Act limiting ownership of land to fifty acres per person. Rich landowners had to give up most their property to the government so the land could be distributed among the poor; families who had no place to call their own could apply for ownership. The socialist Freedom Party instituted a policy of national self-sufficiency, banning the import and export of staples such as white rice, flour, powdered milk and spices and, because this created a demand for staples, rationing the amount each family could buy. People would wait for hours in long queues to buy a loaf of bread or a pound of flour or rice. All the bus routes had checkpoints where police officers arrested anyone who carried more than the allotted amount of food.

The stores stopped carrying imported white rice. I cried when my mother gave me brown rice from our own paddy. Even with my favorite fish curry that rice tasted dry and flavorless. I thought it was a hard life, getting used to eating brown rice and corn instead of bread. A few months later, I learned the true meaning of hardship.

The terrorists rose up against the country when least expected. Unemployed youth and university students formed the communist People's Liberation Front and staged a rebellion against the government, the first ever in

Sri Lanka, setting off bombs and attacking several police stations. Neither the government nor the public knew how to face such a crisis.

The new prime minister, Mrs. Sirimavo Bandaranayake, declared a state of emergency and ordered the elimination of every terrorist. Under the emergency law the military and the police had unlimited power to arrest anyone under suspicion of terrorism, without fear of punishment. Curfew was declared for nighttime, and not a single light was allowed on in homes after six. Lacking the manpower and weapons to fight a battle, members of the People's Liberation Front went into hiding, conducted covert meetings to recruit new members, made bombs and broke into houses looking for weapons.

Thirteen years old at the time, I was traumatized by what was happening. Schools closed. People huddled behind locked doors. My family stayed indoors even during daytime. Every young man and every young woman was a suspect. Military and police officers arrested anyone who was outdoors after curfew and broke into houses to round up more. No proof was needed, and false tips led to the arrest of innocent people.

My innocent little village was turned into a killing field. Military jeeps and trucks were always zooming up and down the gravel road, and at night we would hear bombs going off and shooting in the woods. We watched as orange fire rose from the tree line into the distant sky. Smoke hung in the night air, heavy with the cries of the innocent and with the stench of human flesh set on fire.

Once I overheard my parents talking with a villager who worked as a guard at the Chilaw police station. His words chilled me to the bone. He described heinous torture, particularly of young girls—the police plucked out their fingernails, gang-raped them and beat them until they passed out. They pushed rifles up their vaginal canals and shot them, or broken tonic bottles inside them and watched them bleed to death. I felt sick to my stomach and loathed the police who could do such things.

"Why can't someone complain to the higher authorities?" Amma asked.

"What's the use, madam?" the villager said. "The higher authorities have given them the power to kill on the spot. The military forces are following their orders, using their power to their advantage. This is not the time to confront them. If you go against them, they can kill you right there."

"How long is this going to continue?" Amma pressed.

"They won't stop until they wipe out the People's Liberation Front," he said. "Don't get into any kind of argument or make any enemies, or next thing you know your daughters will be raped and killed."

I was glad that Seetha was far away from Sri Lanka and I feared for Geoffrey, who was still in the mountains, working as a teacher, and from whom I hadn't heard since the onset of violence.

I cried for the victims and felt an urge to help the young rebels fight their battle, and yet I cowered at the sound of a jeep or a truck on the road, dove under the bed and held my breath until long after it had passed.

Weeks and months went by and still, each day, they tortured and killed the young. The death toll mounted until it reached the thousands, and human remains showed up everywhere—bodies floating in the sea and the rivers and lakes of our once-beautiful island, destroying its soul. The only lucky ones were those who landed in jail instead of graves, and those who, after turning themselves in to the police, were hauled off to correctional camps.

The socialist government succeeded in its aim of brutally crushing the People's Liberation Front. When at last the insurrection was over, near the end of 1971, nothing was the same in Sri Lanka. Families didn't breathe a word of their lost ones in public; they held their grief and hatred inside and went about their business. The country resumed the normal business of daily life, but the emergency law stayed in effect for six years, creating haunting memories for all.

Life became a frightening, tiring thing. Village life no longer held any interest for me—the long walk to the road, the salty water and the heat all became a source of irritation. Nor, with Geoffrey off in the mountains, did church interest me anymore. When there I missed his presence and his sweet smile. Out of habit, my fingers would scroll through the hymnal searching for his letter, and the empty pages would just stare back at me. Every breath I took whispered his name. I trusted him completely and believed his love for me was real and untouchable. That was all I ever wanted—someone to love me, just me.

I longed for a change of scenery, and now that I was fourteen I asked Pappa to move me to a school in Negombo. All the best teachers from my convent school had transferred elsewhere, and when, as a result, I started to fall behind in math and physics, it gave my parents a reason to move me to a better school. With encouragement from my godmother, my father's cousin, I was enrolled in the school in Negombo, about thirty miles from Chilaw.

And so a whole new life began. I started living with my godmother, Aunty Neeta, and thereafter came home only for the long holidays.

Chapter 7

Moving in with Aunt Neeta gave me the chance to meet relatives from my father's side. Aunt Neeta, Uncle Alfred and their daughter Dillu lived in a beautiful house near the beach. Dillu was couple of years younger than me and enjoyed having a big sister around. We often visited Aunt Lilli, Pappa's sister, and her husband Uncle Francis, my godfather, who lived a couple of miles away. Uncle Francis stroked my hair and gave me fifty cents or a rupee every time he saw me. They had three children: Swarna, the oldest, who was a teacher and lived far away from home; eighteen-year-old Ivan, who went to a technical school in Colombo; and the youngest, Nimal. On weekends that I didn't go home I went to see Ivan for help with math and physics. I wasn't happy about being tutored by him—I was supposed to be smarter than he was—but I did need help if I was going to compete in my new coed school. To save my pride, the first time I visited him I brought problems I already knew how to do. Despite my reservations we settled into a workable relationship. Ivan never questioned my ability, and with his tutoring I was soon solving problems that had once seemed impossible.

Ivan and I connected quickly and enjoyed our time together. We would play Carom or cards or listen to music. There was just one problem: whenever Aunt Lilli heard me laugh she would peek in the living room and give me the evil eye, or send Ivan off on an errand.

One day I was walking back to Aunt Neeta's after my lessons when it turned windy and gray and rain started to fall. I popped open my umbrella and picked up my pace. Suddenly Ivan came up behind me on his bicycle.

"Hop on, I'll take you home," he said.

"Are you sure?" I said doubtfully, surprised by his sudden appearance. Smiling, he let go of the handle and put his foot on the ground. I hesitated. "Come on, we have to hurry before we get soaked," he said. I arranged myself on the bar in front of him, steadying my books with one hand and with the other holding the umbrella over our heads. His shoulder rubbed against my head as he paddled. When we arrived at my aunt's house, half wet, he dropped me off and turned to leave.

"Aren't you going to come in?" I asked.

"No, I have to go, see you next week," he said and was gone in a flash.

From that day on, Ivan always gave me a lift back to my aunt's, meeting up with me halfway and pretending he was on his way somewhere else. I didn't understand why he was hiding it from his parents; we were cousins and allowed to be together. He also knew about my relationship with Geoffrey. Could he be interested in me? I wondered.

I was writing Geoffrey every week, and in my letters I mentioned Ivan. Geoffrey made arrangements for us to meet at the Negombo train station during a long weekend, and we took the train home together. We hardly spoke to one another, and were embarrassed by the stares the other passengers were giving us, but being close to him was all I needed to feel fulfilled.

A few months later I began to hear rumors about Geoffrey. Some said he was hanging around with another girl. My half-sister Muree who attended the Adventist boarding school, told me about a girl who was trying to get Geoffrey's attention. Probably just another attempt by his mother to destroy our relationship, I thought, trusting Geoffrey completely. In fact, he had told me about this girl, whose name was Ethel, and, I believed, he had been honest with me. In one of his letters he referred to her as "a very smart, talented girl" of whom the other children were jealous. "I feel sorry for her and try to help her," he went on. "She comes to me for advice and the children are fooling around calling our names together." Rather than feeling threatened, I was proud of Geoffrey for sharing this with me, and angry about the rumors.

I decided to question Ivan about his feelings toward me. My relationship with Geoffrey was perfect, I was happy, and I didn't need anyone to complicate things between us. On a church feast day Aunt Neeta, Dillu and I visited Aunt Lilli's house, and while everyone else was in the living room eating and having a good time, Ivan and I sat on the steps outside watching people parade by in their holiday best. It was getting dark, almost time to leave, so I gathered my strength and in a single breath spilled out, "Ayya, are we walking on the same tracks?"

He looked into my eyes with a fleeting expression of sadness. Then his usual serious frown returned. "Nangi, you are my first cousin, and my favorite one. My parents will not let us be anything other than that, even though it is my right. Don't worry, we're on the same tracks. This way I can keep you forever."

I wouldn't dare question him anymore; it felt safe to leave it at that.

"Will you write to me when you go home for the school holiday?" he asked.

"Yes, if you promise to write me back."

"Yes," he said. "Now let's go inside before my mother comes looking for us."

One day a disturbing letter arrived from Geoffrey. "Our love is so innocent," he declared. "We are like the baby animals in the field. We never had any physical contact in our relationship, and we wouldn't hurt each other if we ever broke up. That shouldn't be a disgrace to your character. I don't want to keep hurting my mother, so I've decided to go to India for my studies. I think we should take a little break from each other. Let me know how you feel about this."

I read it over and over, trying to make sure I understood him. He was just testing me, I concluded, and in my reply assured him that he had total freedom to do whatever he wished with his life. But the knot in my stomach belied my conviction that our relationship was still intact. I didn't share any of this with my parents or friends.

During every midyear school break there was a camp meeting at the school in the mountains in Kandy that the Adventists from all over Sri Lanka attended. Geoffrey didn't come home for the break, so I decided to go to the camp meeting to see him. The day before the meeting, I traveled to Kandy with my parents.

"What are you doing here?" my half-sister Muree said as soon as I set foot in her house.

"What do you mean?" I stammered. "You know why I'm here."

She grabbed my arm and steered me into her room. "Haven't you heard? Geoffrey is here with his new girlfriend."

"Girlfriend?" I asked, astonished.

"She is the same girl I told you about; the boys calls her a tramp. Ethel has been after Geoffrey for a long time, somehow she got her hooks into him. Poor Geoffrey is caught up in her web."

Muree's words penetrated like a knife. Her voice was fading, the words growing indistinct, and I sat there trying to collect my thoughts. Presently I wandered out of the house and started running toward the hills. It had to be a rumor. Geoffrey was an honorable boy who would have told me the truth. The only solution was to confront him and hear him say that he didn't love me anymore. Without hearing it from him, I couldn't accept that our relationship was over.

The next morning I went to church and Ethel appeared on the pulpit in a long dress, her pretty hair falling over her shoulders, to sing a solo. She had a full, strong voice that reverberated throughout the church and her eyes focused on the balcony as she sang. My eyes followed her gaze to the balcony, and there he was—my Geoffrey, a proud smile on his face, his eyes locked with hers, nodding to the music. I felt as if I were dreaming. This can't be! I thought. My breathing stopped and my throat was about to burst. No longer able to control myself, I ran out of the church, collapsed on the steps and let out a cry.

Before anyone noticed me, I walked back to Muree's house and stayed indoors. Shame was eating me alive—what would I tell my parents, my friends? What would the world think of me? A sense of deep betrayal seized hold of me. What did this girl have that I didn't? What made him choose her over me? There was only one conclusion I could draw—she was one of them, a Burgher girl.

Fearful that my father might assault Geoffrey, I had to pretend everything was normal until we got back home—and we had a whole week ahead of us. Geoffrey didn't make it any easier for me, walking hand in hand with his new girlfriend with his mother at his side. This advertised their relationship to everyone. Each time I saw them together I died a new death. Rather than confronting him as I had planned, like a coward I hid from him, avoiding any chance of meeting and holding on to the slightest hope that he still loved me. My parents didn't have the time to confront me and the meetings they were attending kept us apart.

I arrived home a different person, feeling betrayed and worthless, hating the world. For six years I had loved Geoffrey faithfully and built up my hopes for a future together. Without him, I thought, there could be no tomorrow. I wrote to him one more time, asking him never to bring such suffering to another woman as long as he lived, and promising him that I would never trust a man again. He never answered.

My world destroyed, I gave up all ambition to be a doctor and sat for long hours under the cherry tree, playing my guitar until my fingers hurt. Despite the hurt, I still loved him and believed that he had been pressured by his mother to end our relationship; that was my only consolation. I felt sorry for him, and imagined that he too was suffering inside for breaking up with me. My love for him was so great that now I wanted to free him so that he could get on with his life. In my ignorance, I decided to prove to Geoffrey that I was over him. And the best way to do that was to marry someone else.

At sixteen, I was too young to think about marriage or ask my parents to arrange it for me. In their eyes, completing my education should be the top priority. But I lost all interest. It was my final year of school and I was supposed to be getting ready for finals, but when I returned to school and opened my books, Geoffrey's face stared back at me. I wanted to punish every boy on earth. I started to look at other boys and flirt with them, but if anyone gave me a note I would take it to the principal and have him punished. Hurting boys was my goal; I didn't care what it did to my reputation. Instead of a sweet, innocent child I wanted to be a wild girl.

News of Geoffrey's betrayal traveled fast, soon reaching every Seventh Day Adventist in Sri Lanka. Pappa—the only person who realized how much I was hurting—was angry, and I had to beg him not to harm the boy. He respected my wish but didn't like what was happening.

During the school vacation I had written a couple of letters to cousin Ivan. One afternoon Aunt Lilli dropped by school, looking for me.

"What's wrong, Aunty?" I said, and she pulled me in to a corner, her eyes burning with anger.

"Are you coming to my house to learn math or to find a man for yourself?"

"What are you talking about, Aunty?"

"You know what I'm talking about, I've been watching you two together, I've seen the way you giggle with him. I didn't bring him up to make a husband to you. Don't you ever set a foot in my house again!"

Holding back tears, I watched her storm off. What had I done wrong? I studied myself in the mirror, wondering why everyone thought the worst of me. Was I a bad person?

That ended my visits to Aunt Lilly. When I told Amma what happened, she was insulted and upset. "Who does she think she is, the queen of England? That her own brother's child is not good enough for her Prince Charming? I will tell your father what his little sister thinks of him."

A couple of weeks later, Ivan dropped by Aunt Neeta's. "Why aren't you coming for your lessons?" he said.

"What? Don't you know what happened?"

"You said you would write from home and you never did, and now that you're back, you don't come for your lessons."

"Ayya, I did write to you! Didn't you receive my letters?"

"No."

"Aunt must have kept my letters from you. She paid me a visit at school and ordered me never to set foot in your house. She thinks I want to marry you."

"Did she say that? I'm so sorry, Nangi. I can't speak for my mother, but you're my cousin, and I don't understand why I can't see you. I want to help you get ready for the finals."

"No, Ayya, I don't need any more trouble. I'm glad I found a good cousin who cares for me, but it's better if you don't come here any more."

"I'll talk to my mother," he said hopefully. I had my own pain to worry about, and no room to bother about his thoughts.

A week later he was back at Aunt Neeta's. Leaning his bicycle on the fence he handed me some papers. "What is this?" I asked without looking at them.

"Last year's exam papers."

"Oh!" I said, disappointed.

"Don't you want to try them? It will help you with your finals," he said.

"I don't want them."

He searched my eyes. "Nangi, if you don't want me to come, I'll respect your wish. Just tell me."

"No, I don't want you to come here any more," I said thoughtlessly. His eyes widened and his smile disappeared. I felt a tiny joy hurting my cousin who had been so good to me.

"I'm sorry, Nangi, I thought you liked me and needed my help. I won't bother you again," he said in a shaky voice, climbing back on his bike. I watched him until he disappeared at the end of our road. Unlike the other times, he didn't look back. The tiny joy turned into pain, and I wanted to run after him and say, *I'm sorry, Ayya, I didn't mean it, please come back!* I had hurt my cousin who would have done anything for me, and I had no spirit left to make things right with him again.

In school, my thoughts took to wandering. Everything on the blackboard was dutifully copied into my notebooks but nothing registered in my head. I hardly heard the teachers' voices, and when it was my turn to answer a question, my friend Kumari who sat next to me always whispered the answer to me.

Kumari was pretty. She had long straight hair worn in two braids, each tied with a red ribbon. And she was rich; her parents had their own house and lived on the same street as Aunt Neeta, a couple of miles from school. We walked to and from school together and became good friends. She told me about her boyfriend and I confessed my secret relationship with Geoffrey. Later when Geoffrey broke up with me, Kumari tried to console me, keeping me company on the weekends, doing my homework and several times rescuing me from the principal's cane. Seventeen years old and in our last year in school, we were still caned by the teachers and the principal for not completing assignments.

Now that I was no longer being tutored by Ivan, I went home for the weekends. Every night under the cherry tree I spilled my heart onto paper, filling page after page with sketches and poems. One evening as I sat there listening to the mosquitoes sing around my ears, the front door opened and a figure approached me in the dark. My father, his hands tucked behind his sarome, came and sat beside me. At first he didn't speak, and when he did it was in a whisper, as if the words might hurt me. "I know you truly loved that boy, but could you still love him? Do you want him back?" Surprised by his question, I mulled it over for awhile. Yes, I decided—I would take him back in a matter of seconds. But I lacked the courage to say so.

When I didn't answer, Pappa said, "If you want him back, I can teach you an exercise to change his mind and he will come back to you."

Pappa never passed on his secrets. I had often wondered why he didn't share his power with any of his children. Now I was amazed to realize that he loved me enough to break this rule. Without waiting for my answer, or maybe before he had any second thoughts, he started to instruct me.

"When you go to sleep at night, take time to relax your body. Lie on your bed and find a comfortable position. Then start to breathe slowly. Listen to the sounds around you, and then try to stop your mind from wandering around; release your thoughts one at a time. Your mind should be free of thoughts, and nothing should disturb you at that point. This will not happen overnight; you have to practice this every night until you get it right." Then he explained how to send telepathic messages to Geoffrey in a state of self-hypnosis. He promised that if I did it right, in a matter of days Geoffrey would come back to me. Neither of us spoke for a minute.

Feeling a sudden need to change the subject, I asked, "Why can't you use your power to be rich, Pappa?" It was a question I had asked myself over and over.

He smiled. "It's wrong to use this power for the wrong thing. I've promised myself never to use it for evil, only for good. Anyone who is gifted enough to gain this power should never misuse it."

"Can you teach me how to gain it?"

"There's so much anger and hate inside you, I would do more harm than good teaching you this."

"I promise never to use it to hurt anyone."

"Prove it to me, child; show me that you can control your feelings."

Excited at the power Pappa had bestowed upon me, I started to follow his instructions closely. But as time went on, I realized that tricking Geoffrey to come back to me was not what I wanted. It had to be of his own free will and because he wanted me. The exercise was useless to me, but Pappa had taught me a good lesson. He had also trusted me to come to my senses before I went too far.

The few weeks I had spent on self-hypnosis had increased my curiosity. I needed to learn more about the power of the mind, and I started to stroll through school libraries and develop an interest in reading books by Sigmund Freud.

One afternoon at Aunt Neeta's, I was playing badminton with my cousin Dillu when I noticed the young man next door standing at the fence studying us. He'd been watching from his front porch every morning when I went to school.

"Nangi, could I please have a few roses from your yard?" he asked my cousin when we switched sides and I was closer to the fence.

"Let me ask my mother," Dillu said and ran inside the house.

The boy threw a folded note into the yard and I picked it up and retreated to the bathroom to read it.

"Could you meet with me after school tomorrow? I will make sure this will not affect your good name in any way," it said, and was signed Berny.

I tossed the note into the toilet and went back to the badminton game. Why did he want to see me? He must be in his twenties, I thought.

After school the next day I was walking home with my friends when I spied Berny following me at a distance. I didn't look back, fearing my friends would notice, and waited until I was alone with Kumari to tell her about the note.

"Why don't you give him a chance?" my friend said. "That's the only way you'll forget about Geoffrey."

We looked back and saw Berny right behind us. Kumari winked at me and started walking away, leaving me alone with him.

Now he was right beside me. "Please, can I talk to you? Let's just walk to the park, and I won't bother you ever again."

My mind was filled with questions. He was handsome; a long thick beard covered most of his face and his eyes seemed kind. Now that I don't have a boyfriend I'm free to talk with anyone I want, I thought, deciding to follow him to the park.

It was the first time I had ever been to a park with a boy, and it surprised me to see the number of couples there. Most of them were schoolchildren with their school uniforms, hiding from prying eyes and lost in their own fantasy. It felt like a different world created only for teenagers. I was embarrassed walking side by side with him, a stranger.

He pointed to a tree a few yards ahead of us and asked me if I wanted to run to it, and I agreed. He counted to three and we both ran. As we reached the tree I bumped into him and fell on the ground, spilling my books all over the grass and laughing. He smiled, helped me up, then gathered my books and gave them to me.

We sat down on a bench surrounded by flowery bushes. "So why did you want to see me?" I asked Berny.

He looked into my eyes and I turned away. "I know you're in a lot of pain," he said gently, "and I want to help you get over it."

"What are you talking about?" I asked, dismayed.

"No one told me anything, so don't worry. All I know is what I can see in you. Did someone break your heart? I would like to listen if you want to talk about it."

"How would you know?"

"I can tell just by looking at you. Your eyes betray the pain you suffer inside."

Lost for words, I tried to hold back the tears, but they fell onto the books in my lap.

"Don't be ashamed to cry in front of me. One tear drop can carry years of grief," he said.

I picked up a leaf and began to break it into bits. He looked at my hands and said, "This is how I read you, by your actions." This time I looked straight at him, our eyes met, and I felt no reason to look away.

"Who are you, and how do you know so much? Are you a hypnotist?"

He smiled. "No, but I can see through people."

Maybe he's like my father, I thought. Suddenly he took my hand in his, but I pulled it away.

"I'm sorry, don't be afraid of me. Think of me as a big brother. I have a girlfriend," he said.

"Then what are you doing here with me?"

"I want to be your friend, a good friend, a brother, whatever you want me to be."

I felt a strange sense of relief, although I had never had a male friend in my life and didn't understand how it was possible for a girl to have male friends. In Sri Lanka, girls associated only with girls.

He showed me a photograph of a pretty girl with long hair falling over one side of her face. He told me that she was from a very rich family, and her parents were against their relationship.

We spent a couple of hours in the park, and I told him about my breakup with Geoffrey, and about how I had taken to flirting with boys and hurting them. He told me that would only make me unhappy.

"You can always love Geoffrey, no one can take that away from you. That's the beauty of love, no one owns it. No one can stop you from loving anyone. But you should stop punishing yourself for loving him and live your life. Make Geoffrey regret it, show him what he lost and make him adore you forever."

It was as if Berny was teaching me a new language. It made perfect sense, and I actually felt happy being with him. By the end of our tryst I promised to see him again, and he promised to guide me in my quest to conquer despair.

From that day forward, Berny and I got together whenever possible. I lied to my aunt every time I left to meet him. Whoever saw us thought we were a couple. Sometimes grownups gave us disapproving looks, and Berny would hold my hand just to watch the expression on their faces. But I regarded him as a brother.

An accomplished photographer, Berny took pictures of me in different poses. He made me laugh and encouraged me to focus on my studies, and I looked up to him for guidance. We went to the beach, the park, the movies. My interest in singing caught his attention. He said I sang just like Neela Wickramasinghe, a Sri Lankan diva. Some days he brought his guitar and played as I sang.

Inevitably, tongues started wagging and the gossip reached my aunt. After school one day I came home to find my mother waiting for me and all my bags packed. She looked angry, but didn't give me a chance to question her because she didn't want to say anything in front of Aunt Neeta.

"I came to take you home. Let's go," she said.

Not daring to question her, I left my aunt's without saying goodbye to any of my friends, not even Berny. Looking back I saw cousin Dillu with her big brown eyes filled with tears chewing on her fingernail. Walking back, I hugged her, kissed her on the cheeks and stepped out of the house.

Amma didn't speak to me all the way home. Then she said, "Your father's very angry this time. Your aunt sent a message asking him to come and get you. She didn't want to keep you in their house any longer, she said that you were a bad influence on her daughter." I could tell from her voice that she didn't approve of what my aunt had done, but she was mad at me nonetheless.

"What did I do wrong?"

"Who is Berny?" Without waiting for my response, she continued. "Aunt Neeta said you were involved with this boy and that the neighbors were talking about you."

"Berny's a friend, he's like a brother to me," I said in one breath.

"Since when is a boy only a friend? Don't you have enough brothers? Why do you need more? I don't know what to do with you. Haven't you learned your lesson from Geoffrey? Why destroy your life and good name with this nonsense?"

It was no use explaining—my mother didn't trust me anymore. Feeling helpless and angry, I waited for my father, hoping he would understand.

But when Pappa came home that night, he didn't even give me a chance to explain. He took me outside and lashed my back with the guava cane, harder this time.

I kept saying, "Berny is only a friend! He helped me get over Geoffrey, please trust me, Pappa!"

It was as if he couldn't hear, he kept hitting me, and finally he said, "You won't go back to Negombo. You'll stay home, study hard and go to the school only for the exams."

I was shaken and angry, even more so because Pappa seemed to have understood me better than anyone else. The disappointment was greater than the pain, and I was up all night.

Morning came, the birds sang, the fields cried and the wind hummed. Pappa left the house at dawn and wouldn't be back for a couple of days. Amma went to town and would not be back for several hours. My sister Milred was at the well taking a shower. It was the perfect time to make my move. I packed a small bag, broke the clay money pot I had kept for several years, sneaked out of the house and ran as fast as my legs would take me to the bus. I was running away—but where?

I decided to go to my friend Kumari's house. I told her what had happened, she covered for me with her parents, and I spent the night at her house.

The next morning Berny came to Kumari's house with my mother. She had been looking for me all night and had gone to Berny's house out of desperation. When she saw me she broke down in tears, begged me to come back home and promised not to say a word to Pappa. I agreed to go. Amma's concern for me melted my heart—her face looked so old and tired—and I felt guilty about hurting her. But I didn't have the courage to ask for her forgiveness.

A couple of months later, I received a telegram from Kumari's sister saying that Kumari had died in an accident. Thinking it was a joke at first, I read the message over and over. Amma thought it was a trick to get me back to Negombo, and when I pleaded with her to let me visit Kumari's home at first she refused. A couple of days later, however, my parents did give me permission to make the trip.

The black flags, the sand on the street and the palms leading up to her house confirmed it. Sick to my stomach, I ran toward the house crying, "Kumari! Kumari!" The house was filled with people and the smell of death chilled the air. I ran into the living room where they would have placed her. In place of her body there was a photo of my dear friend, and candles, lamps and flowers next to her picture. Her relatives were whispering and crying. I went into the kitchen looking for her mother, who uttered a loud cry when she saw me and came running into my arms. "She's gone, you'll never see her again!" her mother cried.

"What happened?" I asked.

"She had an accident and died in the hospital."

All she would say was that Kumari had died in an accident. I sensed that the family was hiding something. Kumari's mother asked me if I knew anything about her boyfriend. I did, but didn't say anything.

Before going back home, I met with Berny and he told me that Kumari had killed herself by jumping in front of a train. She was three months pregnant and no one knew until after her death, not even me. I was horrified, and felt terrible for not being around to support her. She had killed herself to avoid the disgrace she would bring to her family by having a child out of wedlock.

I didn't get a chance to see her—the funeral had taken place the day I received the telegram—and I went home like a ghost, my heart empty.

I thought about what had happened to Ramani, a girl who once lived across the road from us. She was couple of years older than my sister Seetha. After her father passed away, she quit school and stayed home to help her mother in the fields. No one in the village knew she had a boyfriend until her mother found out that she was pregnant. Her mother beat her up mercilessly. Fearing the villagers would kill him, Ramani refused to say who had fathered the baby. Her mother chased Ramani out of the house and told her never to return home. Amma felt sorry for the girl and took her in, then arranged to have her move away from the village, into the home of a friend, Mrs. Silva. Mrs. Silva took care of Ramani until the baby was born, and Amma arranged for the baby to be adopted by another family. Ramani's mother never forgave her, and having no place to go, the girl committed herself to serve Mrs. Silva's family for the rest of her life.

It made sense to me why Kumari had killed herself. Death was easier than living with shame.

That year I didn't make the grades to get into university, and my parents had me take private lessons so that I could repeat the exams. It was the last chance I would have to continue my education, but I had no interest in school anymore. All I wanted was to get away from everything and be on my own.

As if Kumari's death weren't enough, shattering news soon came about cousin Ivan. He had leukemia. All the standard treatments had failed, and his family turned to Pappa for treatment.

In the back of my mind I thought maybe I had brought this upon Ivan—that my hurting him had made him sick. It was imperative that I go to him seeking forgiveness before it was too late. I begged my mother to take me to him.

"Don't you remember what Aunt Lulu told you?" Amma said. "What makes you think that she would let you in her house now? I won't let you be insulted again."

When I asked Pappa he just said, "Don't worry, I won't let him die. I can cure him."

Obviously, arguing with my parents wouldn't get me anywhere. I thought of writing to Ivan, but Aunt Lulu would only keep my letters from him. Perhaps he'll listen to the radio, I thought, and wrote a poem asking his forgiveness. I sent it in to the radio station to be broadcast as a special request.

Each day my father filled me in. "Your cousin has started to walk, he's getting stronger. He's going to be okay," Pappa said with confidence.

But a few weeks later Ivan passed away. Screaming in despair, I pleaded with Pappa to take me with him to Aunt Lilli's, and he did.

When we entered the house it was crowded with relatives, friends and neighbors. Uncle Francis was like a madman. He kept talking to himself, raising his arms up to the sky and crying, "Why didn't you take me instead, why did you pick the best in my family?" Aunt Lilli sat by the coffin caressing her son's head and mumbling to herself. At the sight of me, one of my little cousins started to moan, "Ayya, here is your favorite cousin, she has finally come to see you, open your eyes and see for yourself. You asked me why Ranga Akka"—big sister—"isn't visiting you. She is here, open your eyes, Ayya, open your eyes."

I stood like a statue in front of the casket, in the very same place where we had laughed and worked on math problems together, my throat bursting with the effort to hold back tears. Then I touched his cold hard feet. Forgive me, Ayya, I said silently. He had lost some weight and had no hair, but he looked calm and he was smiling in his sleep. There was no escape; I would live with the guilt for the rest of my life.

Chapter 8

Pappa opened a new clinic in Marawila, a busy town about fifteen miles from Chilaw, and Amma suggested I help out as a receptionist when I didn't have a class. She must have thought that if I worked in the clinic it would rekindle my ambition to be a doctor. Pappa didn't have many patients, and once his appointments were done with he would go off to do odd jobs. I had all the time in the world to feel sorry for myself. I was eighteen and my life had no meaning, so I thought. The pressure from my parents just made it worse. All I wanted was a new beginning.

The clinic was in front of Marawila's main bus stop, and there were always passengers around. Before long I caught the attention of a handsome man with curly hair and a mustache. His hips moved like a woman's when he walked. I smiled at him and encouraged his attention. Soon we became friendly and started to talk. I used a pay phone at the post office to call him at work. His name was Tilak and he was thirty years old, still single and worked for a company that assembled radios in Colombo. He let me borrow his novels and brought me chocolates. I invited him into the clinic when my father was not around and we spent long hours talking. I liked his charm and maturity, and the way he looked at me.

His father had died when he was a little boy, he told me, and he lived with his mother and younger brother and sister. He also had an older brother and sister, both of whom lived close to his town. The family was Buddhist.

My parents would be furious, I knew. First I was involved with an outcast, now a Buddhist man, which was against Adventists regulations.

Tilak seemed like the answer to my prayers. I didn't think far into the future—all I wanted was to be free of my parents and to mend the heart that Geoffrey had broken. Pappa trusted me completely; he had no idea what was happening behind his back.

I didn't know what I really felt about Tilak. I simply enjoyed his company and thought I could love him. When I told him how much I hated living with my parents, he asked me to run away with him. Readily I agreed, and Tilak made all the necessary plans for our elopement. One morning I skipped my class and went with Tilak to the city hall, where his friends were waiting for us.

As an eighteen-year-old I needed my parent's approval to be married, a restriction Tilak navigated around by simply telling the registrar that I was twenty-two. We were married in front of his friends, who signed as witnesses, and then we were off for the town of Bandarawela, in the mountains about a hundred miles southeast of Colombo. Tilak had sent a telegram to my parents that said, "I got married, don't try to find me."

The train huffed and puffed through the thick cool mist as it climbed the mountain, so close to the edge it gave me chills. The sight of the streams took my breath away. The babbling brook and the humming wind joined together and cried sorrowfully among the hills. They're mourning for me, I thought, feeling empty inside despite the excitement of being free from my parents. Sitting next to my husband, I wondered what I was doing with a man almost twice my age. Passing hills green with tea plantations, the train carried me far away into the mountains, toward the new beginning for which I had so often longed.

We went to the home of a friend of Tilak's, Wimal, who worked with him at the radio assembly plant. Wimal had brought his new wife to live there with his parents. Their house was up a hill, at the bottom of which was a bus road and a river where everyone went to bathe and wash clothes.

We spent a week together at Wimal's parents' house. It was my first time being intimate with a man and I had no idea how to act. My eyes filled with tears and I ached with disappointment. At least I didn't have to follow the Sri Lankan custom of using a white bed sheet to prove my virginity to my parents and in-laws.

A week later Tilak went back to Colombo, leaving me and Wimal's wife with Wimal's parents. It was worse than living at home; the couple lived a simple life, ran a small grocery store on their front porch and didn't have enough food to feed us. The cold weather, the baths in the river and the vegetarian meals didn't agree with me. I counted the days and waited for Tilak to come back to me on weekends. That was not the life I had hoped for myself, but it was the perfect place to hide from my parents. They had no idea who I had married and no clues where to search for me.

One day I broke out in a rash and when I went to the doctor, he said I was pregnant. A child of my own, mine to love! Profound joy swept over me; there was no room for grief or regrets. I rubbed my belly and promised my unborn child, "I will love you and be a good mother to you. Nothing in this world will be more important to me than you."

That weekend when Tilak came home, we walked hand in hand along the narrow road toward the center of town. The sun at its crest bathed our bodies in warmth, allaying the effect of the crisp wind. Far away on a hill the train chugged along past misty tea plantations.

Tilak looked happy, and unable to keep my secret any longer, I showed him the rash on my arm.

"What happened?" he said. "Did you get a bug bite?"

"No, it's nothing. Wimal's mother took me to a doctor and he said it'll go away in a couple of weeks."

"Did he say what it is?" he asked with concern.

"Yes," I said, planting myself in front of him and grabbing his hands. Tilak wore his charming smile and his eyes squinted into mine. "Doctor said I'm pregnant!"

I had expected my husband to jump with joy. Instead, he pulled his hands away and the smile disappeared.

"What's wrong?" I said, searching his face. "Aren't you happy?"

Avoiding my eyes, he answered, "I'll take you to Colombo and we'll get an abortion."

"Abortion!"

"You're too young to be a mother. We can wait a couple of years before we have a baby. We have to get rid of this one."

"How could you destroy your own baby?" I cried. "Abortion is illegal in Sri Lanka. If I'm old enough to marry you, I'm old enough to have this baby. Nothing you can say will change my mind!" Trembling with anger, I pushed away from him, crossed the road and climbed down toward the river. Stepping from one rock to another, along the bank, I heard his footsteps right behind me.

"Wait!" he shouted.

I kept walking, but he caught up with me. He took my hand and pulled me down on the rocks. With his arms around my shoulders he turned my head toward him.

"If you don't want this baby, take me back to my parents," I said. "If they won't take me back, I'll find a way to bring it up. No one can take it away from me!"

"I don't want to fight with you over this. Being pregnant isn't easy. Giving birth is even worse. I'll give you a couple of weeks to think about it."

It took Tilak time to get comfortable with the idea of my having his baby, and when he finally did, he made plans to move. A few weeks later we rented an annex close to his workplace in Colombo. He bought everything that was needed for our little house—a bed and a couple of chairs for the one room, and a gas cooker with pots and pans for the kitchen.

It made me feel so grownup keeping house and not answering to anyone. I had often watched Amma cook but had never cooked anything myself. My first day in the kitchen, I burned the rice and poured all the spices I had, including two handfuls of rock salt, into the pan for *dhal* (chickpea) curry. Tilak had brought home some hotdogs which I deep-fried in oil.

Before going to his evening shift, Tilak sat down to eat his dinner. Beaming with pride, I sat down next to him and watched him eat my first cooked meal. I wasn't hungry myself. He smiled at me and continued to eat.

"Is it good?"

"Great," he grinned and continued eating.

Before leaving for work, he kissed me on the forehead and placed some money in my hand. "If you don't feel like eating the food you cooked, go out and buy something you like," he said.

A couple of hours later, having worked up an appetite, I poured some dhal over the rice, took a fried hotdog, sat down at the table, and almost threw up on the first bite. The curry was too salty, the rice tasted like curd and the hotdog was rock hard.

"Oh my God, poor Tilak! How did he eat this?" I muttered, and decided to pay more attention to my cooking.

My pregnancy was an easy one. I didn't suffer much from nausea and didn't crave much, just Amma. I asked Tilak if he could contact her. Instead, he offered to take me to my parents' house.

We took the bus to Chilaw, then a taxi. Tilak, afraid my parents would hurt me, said, "Don't get out of the taxi just yet. I'll go first, talk to your parents and tell them that you want to see them. If they say yes, I'll signal you to come."

Within seconds Amma burst out of the house with a big smile. I got out of the car and ran toward her.

She hugged me and showered me with kisses, crying, "We were so worried about you! I'm glad you came home!"

Pappa kissed me. "What took you so long to come home?"

I was astonished at the way they accepted me after what I had done, shaming the family by running away with a man. Joy crowding out my guilt, I followed Amma into the kitchen. As she put a kettle on the stove I leaned against the door and watched her. "I've been longing to see you and eat your food," I said.

She turned around and looked deep into my eyes. "Are you pregnant?" she asked, and when I nodded she forced a smile and hugged me. I saw the sadness in her eyes, without understanding it.

Amma cooked a special lunch for us, all the dishes I craved, (king fish cooked in black pepper, a special green salad mixed in shredded coconut, fried eggplant salad, spicy beef curry and rice) and I ate up a storm. We were still at the table when Amma turned to Tilak and said, "Let her stay home with us until the end of her first trimester."

Without waiting for him to answer, Pappa said, "There's no question about it, she stays home until the baby is born."

I didn't want to take the control out of Tilak's hands, so I asked him, "Can I stay home for a couple of months?"

Tilak smiled his charming smile and said, "Well, not for the *whole* pregnancy."

"No, just for a couple of months now and a couple of months before the delivery." I kept pleading until he gave in. At the end of that weekend he went back to Colombo, leaving me with my parents and planning to visit every weekend.

I was back home again, but things were different now. No one asked me any questions about my behavior, but I didn't feel comfortable facing the neighbors and I avoided going into town where people would gaze at me with silent mockery. My half-brothers and -sisters, all but Seetha, joined hands with the world and accused me of shaming the family. The Adventist church I loved so much took my name off the membership list for marrying a Buddhist.

The next few months went by quickly, and I tried to be helpful to Amma while learning to cook. My father treated me kindly. He gave me medicine after my first trimester. "This will prevent you from getting any false labor signs, you will only get your labor pain when the baby is really ready to come." Not knowing what he was talking about, I just smiled and took the medicine.

When I went back to our house in Colombo Tilak introduced me to Harriet, a friend who lived next to the company where he worked. I spent time with her family until he got off work, and we became good friends. From Harriet and other friends of Tilak's I learned about the other side of my husband. Apparently he had a weak spot for women. Once I heard this, I started noticing how his handsome looks attracted them, and how he responded. When we were in a crowded bus or train or just walking down the street, Tilak would flirt with other women. It bothered me, but I learned to ignore it.

Sri Lanka is a land of religious freedom where all Buddhist holidays are observed and most major holidays of the other main religions, Christian, Muslim and Hindu. One Buddhist celebration is Poya, a full-moon day marking the beginning of another lunar month. Each Poya represents a different occurrence in the life of Buddha. Buddhist believers spend this day in temples, listening to *bana* (teachings of the Buddha in the Pali language), meditating and observing *sil,* that is, taking a resolution to live by Buddha's precepts. Then in the month of May comes Vesak, which commemorates the birth, enlightenment and death of Buddha. This is the most significant celebration for Buddhist sinhalese.

Being the wife of a Buddhist believer I wasn't able to practice my religion, but I still strongly believed in the Christian God and tried to be faithful to my beliefs. According to my religion it was wrong for me to worship other gods, but it was also my duty to obey my husband. So it was with a guilty conscience that on Vesak, I went with Tilak to his temple in Colombo.

As I entered the temple grounds a whole new world opened up to me, full of chanting *pirith* and *sil observers* dressed in white. No one was allowed to wear shoes in or outside the temple. The quietness and the soft, soothing smell of flowers and burning incense silently embraced my spirit. Tilak guided me to the Buddhu *pilime* (statue) and in a trance I felt myself lighting the oil lamp and laying down lotus flowers that my husband had bought at the entrance. I looked into the face of the statue and a wave of peace broke over me. The sound of chanted mantras hypnotized me and cleansed my soul. I walked around the temple and the grounds watching people meditating, seeking purification.

Outside the temple the moon shone and lanterns strung alongside the road and in front of houses, breathed life into the night. The whole island of Sri Lanka seemed to lie under a spell. All the wrongdoings of mankind were on hold as each person tried to be on his or her best behavior for at least one day. Along the road where crowds were milling small concessions, or *dansal,* offered free food and drink.

We joined Harriet and her family to view the light works in Colombo. Huge *pandals,* lighted screens decorated in various colors and shapes, depicted events from the life of Buddha. We moved with the crowd from one screen to the next, through city streets that had been closed to traffic. Six months pregnant, I held on to Harriet's hand and continued through the crowd.

"Where's Tilak?" I said, feeling tired and searching the faces nearby.

"Don't look back," Harriet whispered suddenly, pulling my hand.

Which, of course, tempted me to do just that. What I saw was unbelievable: Tilak, a few yards behind me, with his arm around a girl's neck and his hand on her breast. My first thought was, didn't he just come out of a Buddhist temple? How could he lose the spirit of purity so quickly?

Harriet blocked my view with her hand and tried to comfort me. "Please don't be upset, it's not good for your baby. He'll change after the baby comes."

Without a word I continued on, my hands sweating. I was surprised by his behavior but it didn't hurt much. The baby kicked me and gently I rubbed my belly. He kicked again against my palm as if needing reassurance, so I whispered, "I'll be a good mother to you, don't worry, my child."

After my breakup with Geoffrey I believed that no man was trustworthy, and Tilak's action seemed to confirm this. But I decided to do my part by being a good wife to him and building a life for my unborn child.

In my third trimester when I went back to my parents' house, Tilak was free to behave however he wanted and I tried not to worry about it. I boasted about my husband to my parents while trying to hide my disillusion. It was a difficult balancing act, but what other choice did I have?

It was dawn when the first sign of labor came. It didn't hurt as much as I had thought it would. I waited anxiously for the pain to get worse. My father reassured me, saying that this was all the discomfort I was going to feel, and he was right—it didn't get much worse. In addition to preventing signs of false labor, the medicine he had given me seemed to be lessening the pain of labor itself. When the contractions started coming closer together, he sent for a taxi to take me to the hospital.

My mother and father took me straight to the check-in counter. The hospital was crowded. The nurse who checked me in said, "It's good to walk when you're in labor. Keep walking until you come to the end of the first corridor, turn left there and walk to the other end and you'll be in front of the labor ward."

We walked to the labor ward and gave our papers to the nurse at the desk. She took one look at me and started to attend to other patients. I was tired and the contractions were intensifying. I kept my hand on my belly and started to rub it gently. Half an hour later I was still standing at the nurse's desk waiting for my bed. Other pregnant women close to their delivery were crying and yelling with pain, and I was terrified. Pappa saw the expression on my face and asked the nurse at the desk to take me to the delivery room.

"Isn't this her first baby?" she asked. "She's not in pain. I don't think she's going to deliver today."

Pappa whispered in my ear, "You'd better start crying, pretending you're in pain—otherwise you're going to deliver the baby right here!" Then he turned to the nurse. "Shouldn't you check her before you make an assumption about her delivery time? She's in labor, you have to take her to the delivery room now!"

The nurse gave my father a dark look, then steered me to a bed. I guess she wanted to prove him wrong, but Pappa was right. I was in labor and she didn't even have time to change my clothing before rushing me into the delivery room. My parents had to wait outside.

She took me inside and I was laid on a bed. A midwife and a nurse's aide came to my bedside and tried to encourage me with the delivery, asking me to keep pushing. They were surprised that I wasn't in pain. Soon a lady doctor came in and stood in front of me.

"Do you think having a baby is so simple? Push hard now! Now!" she yelled, and I gathered all my strength and pushed. Suddenly it felt as if a sharp blade were going through my flesh, cutting me, and I screamed at the top of my lungs. There was a baby's cry and I heard someone saying, "It's a boy," and I laughed through my tears. The nurse put a bed sheet over me and took the baby, washed him and deposited him in a crib out of sight. I heard his cry and ached to hold him in my arms. They left me on my bed soaking wet, still bleeding from the episiotomy, wondering why they'd had to cut me and why they hadn't stitched me up yet. Six long, painful hours later a nurse came into the room and started to clean me.

"Why did she cut me?" I asked her.

"Is this your first child?"

"Yes."

"Well, it's a new law. We have to cut for the firstborn," she said.

A while later the doctor who delivered the baby came to stitch me up. I thought she would inject medication to numb the skin beforehand, but she didn't. As the needle dug into my flesh I held onto the bars on the headboard and screamed. Two nurses held me down to stop me from moving.

When it was all over I had no strength left in me. The nurses changed my clothing and took me to another ward along with my son.

One look at Samadha and I forgot my suffering. He looked just liked his father. As I held him in my arms and tried to teach him to take his first meal, warm love surged through me and I knew I had a reason to live.

Amma was the happiest of all. I had given her first grandson. Tilak visited me at the hospital, proud to have a son. I stayed in the hospital for three days before going home to my parents.

Amma took care of me until my body healed. She wrapped my stomach with two yards of fabric to shrink it to its original size, washed the wound with hot water and pumped milk from my breasts to ease the discomfort. She taught me how to care for my newborn while she did most of the caring. All I did was feed him. Even at night when he woke up crying, Amma would put him next to my breast, wait until he was full, then change his cloth diaper and rock him back to sleep. She made a cradle out of her sari and hung it from the roof to rock Samadha to sleep, then laid the sleeping child next to me on the bed. In Sri Lanka, a baby always sleeps in its parents' bed.

When I finally went back to live with Tilak in Colombo, Samadha was six months old. We had moved into an annex next door to the landlord. The landlord's three daughters visited all the time and helped me with the baby. This would have been a great help, except that the oldest girl, Samira, suffered from some kind of personality disorder. She must have inherited it from her mother, who, when possessed, had red eyes and a big tongue hanging down. The mother abused her children and mimicked her deceased mother, who had walked with a limp. Neighbors whispered that Samira was possessed by the Black Prince, a devil who inhabited virgins when they were left alone after sunset during menstruation. Once a girl was possessed by the Black Prince she would hear him calling. Sometimes, hearing a drum from the nearby temple, Samira would start dancing and messing up her hair, then rip off her clothes and run after the sound. Whenever she was in this trance she possessed superhuman strength and no one could control her. The sight of her dancing and tearing down the road made the hair on my skin rise, and I grew so afraid that even when she was normal, I didn't want to look at her or let her into the house, much less go to sleep when I was alone. Eventually Tilak and I moved to another house.

Tilak was good to me in all ways but one: his dalliances continued. I heard gossip that one of his paramours was his boss's wife. Strangely enough, it didn't hurt much. I had a perfect son, I reasoned, and he was everything to me. Fighting with Tilak, moreover, would only make life miserable for Samadha. I decided to tolerate my husband's behavior as long as he was good to my son and me.

Before long Tilak lost his job at the radio assembly plant and took me to live with his family. Tilak's sister and brother still lived with their mother at the time. It was a huge old house built on five acres by Tilak's grandparents. All kinds of fruit grew there—mango, papaya, cashew, jackfruit, coconut, oranges, grapefruits and various spices. They owned coconut groves and rice paddies, and though they came from a higher caste than my family, earned a good income from their land and lived in relative comfort, theirs was a simple Buddhist life—the life of rural villagers. They didn't wear fancy clothes or jewelry, and looked at me as if I was from another planet when I wore dresses and put makeup on my face. Being with them made me uncomfortable, and I didn't want to live the life that was expected of me, laboring in the fields.

Thinking it would be much better if we moved in with my parents, I began making my case with Tilak and eventually convinced him. That's when the trouble started.

Ever since the family had come together during the celebration of my coming of age, all of my half-sisters and brothers visited my parents. It was my first Christmas with the family since marrying Tilak and, wanting to look nice, I slipped into an attractive dress and arranged my hair with matching pins. I ran into Tilak in the front yard. One look at me and his face turned beet red.

"Why are you wearing that short dress?"

Confused, I said, "What's wrong with this dress?"

"You're not a little girl anymore," he yelled. "You can't wear that dress. It shows your legs. And take off those clips and put your hair up. You're a mother now—dress like one and act like one." A boy paddled by the house on a bicycle, staring at us. He must have heard the yelling.

"Why is that boy looking at you?" Tilak snapped. "Do you know him?"

"No, I don't."

"Then why is he looking at you?"

"How do I know? What's the matter with you—don't you trust me?"

He walked away muttering to himself. Bewildered by his behavior, I went inside and changed into a long skirt and a blouse. My mother didn't like what I was wearing but I pretended that it was what I wanted to wear. I tried to stay calm and enjoy the day with my family. Tilak spent most of it in the backyard, avoiding the visitors. He felt as uncomfortable around my family as I did around his.

Tilak began to fight with me over little things. I didn't want my parents to know we were fighting, so I took him into the woods whenever I had to explain things to him.

He refused to find a job and stayed home waiting for my family to provide for us. I decided that it was time for me to find a job, and started taking typing lessons. Tilak followed me to make sure that I would not talk to any men and would come straight home. He was always after me, buzzing like a bee with his complaints, trying to draw me into an argument. He hovered over me and didn't give me any space.

Tilak wanted me to come and live with his mother but I refused. I asked him to find a job and rent a house so we didn't have to live with anyone. Unable to come to an agreement, we parted ways temporarily. He went to live with his parents and stopped visiting as frequently. My parents, seeing what was happening, were very upset. They stood by me and suggested that I stay with them until he found a job and a place for us to live.

One day Tilak came for a visit, took Samadha to the store to buy him candy and didn't return home. A couple of hours went by and I grew alarmed, thinking something awful had happened to both of them. I walked down the road with Amma, questioning every passerby. No one had seen them. I went to shops near the bus stop and asked if they had seen Tilak with our son, and no one had. Without wasting time waiting for a bus, we walked to town and searched there. No sign of them.

"Amma, how are we going to find Samadha?" I said, trembling with fear.

"Tilak must have taken him home. Why don't you go to his mother's house and look?"

"To his mother's house, without me? Why would he do that?" I tried to picture Samadha at Tilak's house. He was only a year old and I didn't think he could spend one hour without me. He must be terrified, I thought.

"If he's not with Tilak, come back home. We have to inform the police," Amma said.

I boarded a bus, then realized that I was barefoot and in my home clothes, but it didn't matter. When I reached Tilak's home I heard my son crying, calling for me, "Ammy, Ammy!" I ran inside and when he saw me he ran into my arms screaming. I kissed his scared face and held him close to my chest. Infuriated with Tilak, I was nonetheless hesitant to take a stand, knowing I had to protect my son and not lose him. And so I played it safe.

"Why did you bring him here without telling me?" I asked when Tilak's mother wasn't around.

"I knew you would come looking for him. I want you to live here with me, not with your parents," he said.

"Living here means living with a parent, so what's the difference?"

"Part of this land belongs to me; I can build a house for us. Until I do that we can stay here."

"Why can't I live with my parents where I'm comfortable until you build that house?" He laughed, and I realized there was no point in arguing with him.

I stayed at his mother's for a few days to convince him that I still wanted to live with him.

A few weeks later Tilak allowed me to go back to my parents until he found a job. I waited patiently for him to keep his promise, but he remained unemployed. A few months later Tilak took off with Samadha again. This time Pappa didn't let me go after him; instead he went to the police. The police didn't find my son at Tilak's house. Amma and I searched for him high and low, appealing to friends, relatives, everyone who knew Tilak, but it was useless.

"He is the child's father so we can't do much," the police told me.

"I am his mother and he needs me more than his father. I still breastfeed him—how can his father take care of him?"

"We will try to find him, and if we do we can warn him, but legally there's nothing we can do."

With every passing hour I grew more frantic, feeling the fear and longing in Samadha's heart. After three weeks of agony, finally Pappa found him at Tilak's sister's house, where he had been living while Tilak remained at his mother's house. When Pappa brought him home to me Samadha's eyes seemed sad and lifeless, he was confused, and his body was covered with a rash and bug bites. Not only did he not smile—he didn't even cry. It was awful not knowing had happened. My only consolation was having him back in my arms where he belonged.

Nothing changed between Tilak and me. My son was about two years old when my parents received news that Tilak was having an affair with a friend of mine. They were shocked and furious. Amma started to blame me, reminding me that it was my choice I was in this mess. Now they knew the truth. I felt so ashamed that I couldn't face my parents or deny Tilak's actions. Wanting to escape all the emotional upheaval for awhile, I took a handful of sleeping pills and lay down.

I woke up in the hospital, and when I tried to sit up I felt drowsy and fell back on the bed. I recognized the nurse's aide at my bedside, an old friend from school.

"Do you remember me, Ranga?" she said.

"Yes. Aren't you Tikiri?"

"I'm glad you remember me. Your mother brought you to the hospital just in time—why did you want to kill yourself?"

"I didn't," I replied quickly, unable to keep my eyes open. My mind was drifting. "I only wanted to sleep for a while without thinking... What's wrong with me? Where's my son?"

"Calm down, Ranga, I'm only trying to help. The hospital staff thinks you tried to kill yourself, so they had to inform the police. The police can lock you up if they believe this is a suicide attempt."

"But it isn't!" I said, alarmed. "What should I do?"

"When the police officers question you, don't tell them that you took sleeping tablets. Tell them that you had a headache and took some tablets and that you didn't know they were sleeping tablets. I know most of the policemen and I'll talk to them, but be careful what you say."

Thanks to Tikiri and my mother, the police didn't arrest me. But I had other things to worry about. By the time Amma returned home from the hospital, Tilak had taken Samadha again. Milred, who had been watching Samadha, had no power to stop Tilak, and Pappa was visiting my sister Seetha in Pakistan. This time Amma would have to fight my battle.

I hated Tilak for tearing my heart apart, over and over. Too drowsy to function, I had to spend several days in the hospital, agonizing over Samadha's fate. The longer I was delayed, the longer he would suffer. I was ready to settle it once and for all. While I tried to recover from my overdose, my mother went back to the police. She filed a complaint and begged them to find Tilak. Since it was the third time Tilak had done this, the police officers were now on my side. They searched for him and sent him a message to report to the police station with Samadha.

He did report in, and after being released from the hospital I spent a day at the police station speaking with Tilak face to face in front of an officer. I spilled everything, explaining to the officer that Tilak was a womanizer and that I couldn't go back to him, and why our son would be safer with me. Tilak denied everything but agreed to leave us alone. He was forced to bring Samadha back to me and was given a warning.

My temporary stay with my parents became permanent. Too embarrassed to go to court and be stigmatized by getting a divorce, I stayed married to Tilak for several more years, but he stopped dropping by my parents' house. For all practical purposes, the marriage was over.

Amma said it was my fate to live at home. I decided it was time to find the courage to face my shame and grow up—to earn my own living and free my parents from this burden. I went looking for jobs, but it was impossible to find a decent one without more education.

That's when a friend of mine told me about an agency that sent young Sri Lankan women to Middle Eastern countries to work as maids. My parents didn't like the idea of my being a servant in another country, but I was so desperate to free them from their burden that I decided to give it a try.

And so I went to the agency and met the man named Barla. According to him, the women he sent to Lebanon made good money and were happy.

"How much do they make in Sri Lankan rupees?" I asked.

"About two thousand a month," he said. "If you save it all, in two years you will come home with forty-eight thousand rupees."

"Oh!" I held my breath, trying to imagine what I could do with that kind of money. There was no way I could ever make that much working in my country.

"How soon can you send me to Lebanon?" I asked.

"I'll get the papers ready in a couple of weeks. You have to sign a two-year contract, and I need your passport and two photographs." He paused. "My charge would be five hundred rupees."

Where am I going to find five hundred rupees? I wondered, but it sounded like a good opportunity. I went home, discussed it with my parents and got their approval. Amma agreed to borrow the money from a friend, and I promised to pay her back with interest.

And then I flew to Lebanon.

PART III

AGAINST ALL ODDS

Chapter 9

Off Lisha's balcony I was falling, the cold wind was pushing hard against my body and I was struggling to breathe. As darkness engulfed me I heard myself scream. Then someone's arms were around me and I felt as though I were flying. Without fear, and with my mind at peace, I closed my eyes.

Whispers started in my head, growing louder until they turned into voices all around me. Where am I? I wondered. My eyelids were heavy and swollen and I tried to open them, wincing in the strong light. Gradually, faintly, as if seen through a veil, the form of a beautiful angel took shape beside me. Is this a dream, I thought, or am I dead? Widening my eyes, I tried to focus. That's when I saw Lisha's daughter Jena. She was marching back and forth and in a flash I was back, with a clear memory of jumping off the balcony.

Alive, I'm alive!

My joy was cut short by a sudden fear: If Jena was here, Lisha must be close by. What were they doing here?

Maybe I didn't have any severe injuries and they had come to take me back. Suddenly I couldn't breathe, my vision was doubling and I gasped for words. I had to tell someone not to send me back there! I looked at the angel's face. She was leaning over me, her lips moving, but I couldn't hear her. Shaking uncontrollably, I tried to speak but my throat hurt and nothing came out. Suddenly I heard myself yelling, "Don't send me back there, she's going to kill me! She's going to kill me!" Then everything went blank.

When I opened my eyes again I was fully conscious. Two gentlemen were standing by the bedside. I recognized their uniforms—they were police officers. After all the weeks of hoping that the police would save me, the sight of them now made me uncomfortable. In Sri Lanka, if you survive a suicide attempt they send you to jail. I had no idea what the laws were in Lebanon, but the appearance of the police made me think that maybe I would be put in jail. I tried to listen to what they were saying, but I couldn't understand anything.

"Don't tell them the truth," someone whispered in my ear. It sounded like Mr. Zain, and my eyes searched for his face. I have no recollection of what happened next.

"Are you awake? Can you hear me?" A gentle voice touched my heart.

I opened my eyes and looked into hers. She had a pretty round face and short, straight black hair. When she smiled her eyes smiled with her. It was the most comforting vision I had ever seen. I tried to speak but had no voice, and instead just blinked. She understood me. Tears filled my eyes and when I tried to wipe them away, a sharp pain in my back stopped me. "Don't move," she said, sitting down beside me and wiping my tears, "and try not to speak. You're in a hospital, in case you were wondering. You fell from the balcony on the fourth floor. The doctors performed surgery as soon as you were brought in. You've been in and out of consciousness for twenty-one days. This is the first time you're conscious, so try not to use your energy to speak. The best thing for you now is to rest. When you are strong again, the doctors will fill you in."

She stroked my hair gently. "I have to leave now. I'm going to church tonight, and I'll pray for you."

I tried to speak again, and she bent forward to listen to what I was saying. Her ears were almost touching my lips, and I could smell her sweet flowery skin.

"Could you light seven candles for the Holy Spirit?" I murmured. It took all the strength I had in my body to utter those words.

"It would be my pleasure to do that for you. I know the Holy Spirit will help you," she said, and left.

I drifted back to sleep and when I woke up again it was night, and I was alone. My body felt so stiff that I was afraid to move. A curtain surrounded my bed and I couldn't see anything beyond it, though whispers were audible from outside the room. Machines were hooked up to me. IVs were attached to my arms, an oxygen tube ran through my nose, and a huge tube ran under my shoulders and into a big glass bottle beside the bed. A white blanket covered me from my waist down. I tried to move my legs, but there was no feeling. In fact, there was no feeling whatsoever from the waist down.

Footsteps approached, then the curtain moved and a nurse came in. When she saw me, her eyes widened and she smiled. "Oh! You're awake. How are you feeling?"

"Happy..."

"Happy? That's wonderful. I'm going to give you a shot to ease your pain." She moved the blanket and gave me a shot in the arm. Then she emptied my catheter.

"You're a lucky girl—do you know that?"

Responding with a smile, I thought, if only she knew what I had to go through to be lucky.

She held my right arm and showed me the button that was taped to my palm. "If you need anything, press this button and someone will come to you."

Again, I responded with a smile.

Then she replaced the blanket, turned off the light and left.

Awash in the joy of freedom, I couldn't go back to sleep that night. I had escaped! Then I remembered the police and what Mr. Zain had whispered in my ear. What did he mean by not telling the truth? Did he know what had really happened? Why had the police been here? Had I said anything while I was unconscious?

Again I thought of the law in Sri Lanka: If you survive a suicide attempt they send you to jail. Was it the same in Lebanon? Having escaped from one prison, I didn't want to land in another.

I was happy to be alive and free from Lisha, but I had to be careful of what I said to anyone. Now that the misery was behind me, I had to play it safe until I got out of the country. Keeping the secret to myself seemed like a safe choice.

In the early morning I fell asleep and dreamed about running around and playing with Samadha. Later that morning three doctors and the woman with the angel face greeted me. I smiled cheerfully at them.

"How are you feeling, Patricia?" one of the doctors asked.

"My name is not Patricia; I'm Ranga," I said.

"That's the name that was given to us. I'll call you Miss Suriya. Tell me how you feel?"

"Strong," I said.

"That's good," he said. "I'm Dr. Marwan. This is Dr. Basen—" he pointed to a short young man, who nodded "—and this is Dr. Assad." Dr. Assad was a tired-looking middle-aged man whose lips, when he smiled in greeting, stretched all the way across his cheeks.

"Do you remember what happened to you?" Dr. Marwan asked.

"No." The word jumped out of my mouth before I could think.

"Well, you fell from the fourth floor. You were lucky the guards found you soon enough to bring you to the hospital. The fall fractured your spine. The spinal column is broken. Three bones were badly damaged. We've performed surgery to avoid internal damage, but we have to wait until you're stronger to work on your spine." He paused, then spoke in a gentler voice. "The damage to your spine has paralyzed you from the waist down. We're going to do the best we can, but we don't think you'll ever walk again."

There was silence. It took me a while to absorb his words. The faces before me were grave, looking as if they had suddenly stopped breathing and turned into statues. I closed my eyes and felt the tears running down to my ears.

Paralyzed. Never walk again. The words echoed in my head. My throat was closing up and my lips were trembling.

"It's a miracle you're alive. You should be happy about that," Dr. Marwan went on.

A miracle! Of course. I was alive, that was a miracle, and if one miracle could happen, why not another? I *would* walk again. God had shown me a miracle. He wouldn't let me live to be an invalid.

I came alive with hope, with the joy of God's love. My trust in Him was fully restored, and it filled me with determination. "Don't feel bad for me, Doctor. I'm going to walk again."

The doctors looked at each other and then at me with disbelief. Dr. Basen said, “It’s good to have faith in yourself. We’ll do whatever we can, but we can’t give you false hope.”

The beautiful woman came closer. Her eyes looked sad, but there was a hint of hope in them that encouraged me. Her hand felt warm in my palm and I closed my eyes to hold on to my strength, to find the courage God had given me.

After the doctors left, she said, “My name is Nasya. I’m your physiotherapist.” She pulled up a chair and sat beside my bed. “I’ve helped patients walk before, and I promise to help you walk again.”

For the first time in a long time, someone was on my side.

Suddenly I had an urge to see my legs. “Can you please show them to me?” I said.

She went to the foot of the bed, folded the blanket to my waist and lifted my legs slightly, holding them in her palm so I could see them. There was no sensation of warmth from her palms. My legs had no feeling and they looked different, ugly and lifeless, with flaky skin and big red spots on either side of the heels.

“How did I get those spots?”

“Your legs have been in the same position for so long that the blood has started to clot. It will go away once you start moving,” she said, covering my legs back up with the blanket. “Keep your courage; together we’ll overcome this. No matter what the doctors say, don’t lose your faith.”

That day, for the second time in my entire life, I felt blessed. The first time was the day I was baptized as a Seventh Day Adventist. I was only eight years old at the time, too young for baptism in the Seventh Day Adventist faith, but I cried and begged my father and the pastor until they gave in to me.

It was during a camp meeting that I was baptized. I came out of the water feeling God's presence in me. That whole day I kept repeating to myself and to everyone who greeted me, "Jesus is with me now, Jesus is with me now!"

Now I felt the same glorious joy and believed that He was there to watch over me. God was the only thing I had to give me the strength to face reality.

Lying helpless twenty-four hours a day is one of the most difficult things a person can do. I had all the time in the world. My paralysis was only from the waist down, but the muscles in my shoulders and arms had grown so weak from surgery and lack of activity that I was unable to move even my hands. I couldn't wipe my own tears, let alone hold them back. Someone had to help me with all my physical needs.

The first few days of consciousness were dreadful. I slept most of the day and was up at night. My hands were swollen, and the needles made sore bruises on my arms and legs. The nurses had a hard time finding a clean vein on my arms. All the veins had been used and reused, and they throbbed with pain.

One night I woke up, saw the empty saline bag, and watched in terror as the last drop ran down to my body. I wanted to scream to alert the nurse, but my voice had no strength. I could feel the button on my palm, but my wrist was too swollen with the IV needle and I couldn't move my fingers to press it. There I lay, helpless, hoping someone would come in. The seconds ticked by, and blood started to suck back into the saline bag. Thankfully the head nurse dropped in to check on me.

"Allah! No one checked up on you? Oh, my poor child, I'm so sorry!" she said. She replaced the saline bag and promised to keep an eye on me, then left the room and began yelling at the nurses.

Visiting hours were the worst. I lay on my bed helplessly, watching and listening to the voices of people visiting other patients, desperately longing to be with my family. Since I was unable to move my hands I had asked Nasya, the only person I could trust, to write a letter to my parents. When was I going to hear from them?

Within a few days, I was taken off the machines and the tube was removed from my back. They moved me to a room with another patient. I still slept most of the time. Nasya dropped by every day for our physical therapy sessions, which gave me something to look forward to. For a while she was my only visitor and friend. She comforted me like a mother, supported me in my faith, and strengthened me with her care. Truly, she was an angel sent by God to watch over me.

Time crawled by, and there was nothing I could do to pass it. A few seconds felt like a lifetime. With my body still in shock and my arms still unable to hold a book or write a letter, all I had were my thoughts to keep me company. I began to feel like hospital furniture.

I tried to establish some semblance of routine to keep my mind busy. Gradually the daily routine at the hospital became a part of my life. I woke up early in the morning, long before the nurse's first round. When she did come around I would greet her with a big smile, the only thing I could offer. She would check my blood pressure and temperature, then inject my medication. As she continued with her rounds the soft whispers, moans and complaints of the other patients reached my ears.

While able patients began their morning wash up, I silently prayed to God, asking for strength to believe in myself and to hold on to my dream of walking again. Then I would sing, softly at first, then with a rising voice:

> My faith looks up to Thee,
> Thou Lamb of Calvary, Savior divine;
> Now hear me while I pray,
> take all my guilt away,
> O let me from this day be wholly Thine.

No one complained about my singing or tried to stop me, and I continued to praise the Lord with hymns until I was filled with joy.

One morning, just before breakfast was served, two nurses came to my bedside. "It's time to wash you up," one of them said, beginning to undress me. I was ashamed of being naked and helpless in front of them. The other nurse soaked a washcloth in hot water and wiped my body down, which relieved my itching skin. She tickled me as if I were a child and pulled my nipples. It was humiliating, but she was only trying to be nice.

"Your skin is like chocolate," she said, and began to call me Chocolat. Then they sponge-bathed my body with huge bottles of cologne. It felt so refreshing to smell like something other than medicine.

"The cologne will protect you from bedsores," the nurse said, sprinkling powder all over my body.

Finally, dressed in a fresh hospital gown, hair brushed, mouth washed, I was clean.

The nurses were very gentle with me, but still it hurt to be moved. What hurt the worst was when they changed the bedding and moved me from side to side. Then I screamed with agony.

"I know it hurts you, Chocolat, and I'm sorry, but I have to change the sheets," said the nurse as she wiped my tears. "You never give us any trouble, I wish all the other patients could be like you."

Before long I got to know all the staff at the hospital and became friends with everyone. Their voices, footsteps and even their touch had become so familiar that I could recognize them with my eyes closed. At night the head nurse, Enid, and the others would come to chat and share the intimate details of their lives with me. We laughed and joked way into the night.

Making friends with the patients who shared my room was easy. Unfortunately no one stayed long, one or two days, at most a week. But they always came back to see me, and I started receiving a stream of visitors. The people who visited other patients also began stopping at my bedside. The visitors brought me flowers, food and books, read to me and wrote letters to my family.

While still waiting impatiently to hear from my family, I was growing stronger, thanks to all the help. One day I was taken off the IVs and started on solid food. This was extra work for the hospital staff, but my visitors pitched in when they were around, feeding me themselves.

Some nights I woke up with a dry mouth, sweating and in need of water. Unable to reach the water beside my bed, I would wait in the hope that a nurse would check up on me. Ringing for the nurse in the middle of the night didn't feel right, so I tried to resist the temptation, but sometimes it was too much and after a long wait I would ring the bell for help.

"I'm sorry to disturb you, but I can't go back to sleep, I need some water."

"That's alright, Ranga, don't feel bad. I know you won't bother us if you can help it," she said, feeding me water by the spoonful.

A couple of weeks later, Nasya decided that it was time to start working on my upper body. She turned me onto one side and left me there for a few minutes. The weight of the bones pressed painfully against the muscles, which had no strength to hold them. The pressure squeezed my heart and as I held onto the bed rail for support I was breathless, with tears pouring out of me, soaking into the pillows. Ignoring the pain, I began to sing. After that day, whenever I was in agony, or gloomy or lonesome, I sang to overcome the misery. Despite the will to be strong, however, my spirit weakened at times. The possibility of never walking again scared and depressed me.

"Do you remember what happened to you, Ranga?" Nasya asked me one day. For a second I thought of telling her the truth, but something stopped me.

"I don't remember," I said abruptly.

"Did Lisha push you off the balcony?" Nasya asked, and I looked into her eyes, not believing what I'd heard.

"Why do you say that?"

"That's what I heard. Is it true?"

Why would anyone think that Lisha pushed me off the balcony? I wondered. Did I say anything while unconscious? Did they find the note in my uniform pocket? I didn't know what to think. She was waiting for an answer.

"She was mean to me," I said, "but she didn't push me."

"The first time you were conscious, you became very upset and kept saying she was going to kill you. When the police questioned you, you didn't remember anything."

"I remember the police being here, but I can't remember talking to them."

"You were in and out of consciousness those days, but I saw the terror in your eyes when you saw Lisha's daughter. That's why I thought the rumors were true," she said.

"What was Jena doing in the hospital?" I asked.

"Lisha came to the hospital with her daughter. Mr Zain was there too, they all wanted to know what you were going to say to the police." Nasya paused. "Would you go back to her when you're released from the hospital?"

"No! Can they really send me back to her?"

"I don't know, but where would you go?"

"Home, to my son," I said quickly.

"Once you're released from the hospital, you'll need someone to take care of you. You can't be alone. If Mr. Zain can't provide you that care, the hospital might release you to Lisha."

"Please don't let them send me back to her!" I cried, feeling sick to my stomach.

"You're not going anywhere anytime soon, so don't worry about it," said Nasya.

Going back to Lisha was a terrifying thought, and the next time Nasya came by I told her how the woman had abused me and how I had tried to escape by unlocking Lisha's door. But I didn't breathe a word about how I had really escaped.

From that day on, if anybody questioned me about Lisha, I told how she had tortured me. Visitors who had become my friends were sympathetic. Some offered to take me into their homes and care for me, some asked for Lisha's address and said they would kill her for doing this to me. What would have become of me if I had had the chance to work for one of these nice people? I wondered.

Mr. Zain never visited me at the hospital, but his secretary, Marcia, did. On her third visit, about a month after I was hospitalized, she brought me some letters from home. Screaming with joy, I read the letters out loud. They were old letters, written while I was trapped in Lisha's house. It was painful to read one of Amma's letters: "What has happened to you, duwa (daughter)? We have not heard from you since you said goodbye. This mother's heart knows when one of her children is in trouble. I know something is wrong. Please hang on to your faith, we will do whatever it takes to find you."

"Why didn't you send these to me as soon as you received them?" I asked Marcia.

"We did give your parents' letters to Lisha. I don't know how we missed these; I only found them last week hidden between some files," she said.

There was no reason to fight her. Besides, I had already mailed several letters to my parents telling them that I was in the hospital. They would be receiving them soon.

At the time of my hospitalization civil war was raging in Beirut, between the Muslims and the Christians. Often we heard the sound of bombs exploding nearby and windows shattering. The injured were being rushed into the hospital. No patients were allowed out onto the balcony. The nurses assured me the hospital was safe, but I had to wonder what would happen if a bomb hit the building—what would my chances of survival be then, without legs to run? War, however, was the least of my fears. I had lived through it at the age of thirteen, and though nothing could be worse than what I had seen and heard about, the fact that I had survived it—and survived Lisha—fed my courage.

Nasya continued to comfort and encourage me in every way. One time she invited some of her other patients to visit me. They were all victims of the war, most of them cripples. Some walked with a limp. Some had lost body parts. It was a disturbing sight and I pitied them.

"These are all people who thought they would never walk again," Nasya said with a smile. "They had to work hard to get to this stage, but it's worth it."

How could I tell her that I didn't want to be a cripple? If I walked again, I wanted to look normal so that no one would ever know that anything was wrong with me.

Frightened and discouraged, I cried that night and begged God for guidance.

Early the next morning I woke up needing to empty my bladder. It felt as if it were going to burst. This was the first time I'd had such a feeling since the fall. When I rang for the nurse, Enid walked in.

"I need to do number one," I told her.

"You do? That's great that you can feel it; maybe we can take you off the catheter. Let me check with the doctor," she said, emptying my catheter and relieving my discomfort.

That day I began to use the bedpan, and in about a week's time Dr. Assad announced that my body had started to heal, that all of my internal organs had started to function normally. He also said that I would be able to bear more children. The news lifted my spirits, and I spent the whole day singing.

As my body gained strength, Dr. Marwan decided it was time for me to have a second operation. When they got me ready for surgery I was filled with fear. Comforting words from patients and visitors didn't help. Someone offered me his portable phone to call my parents, but my parents didn't own a phone—they didn't even live close to a family with one. I cried like a baby as they moved me into the operating room, desperate for my parents.

Underneath the huge lights, surrounded by doctors and nurses, I listened to my heartbeat. Doctors and nurses surrounded my bed, their faces hidden behind surgical masks and gowns, looking like aliens. A nurse tried to comfort me before they gave me anesthesia.

Hours later I was wheeled back to my room. The movement of the gurney made me groan in agony. Every stitch on my back hurt; it felt as if I were lying on a bed of knives. When they lifted me off the gurney and placed me on the bed, the pain was so severe that it felt as if my back had been ripped open. I screamed until my throat hurt, then passed out and slept for many hours while they monitored my every breath.

The surgeons had fused my fractured bones, attaching two Harrington rods to my spine for support and doing a bone graft from my left hip. Unbearable pain was the price I paid for being able to feel my upper body. If anyone approached me I screamed, anticipating the pain if the bed was accidentally bumped.

"Keep everyone away from me—no visitors, please!" I begged the nurses. All I wanted was to be left alone.

Chapter 10

By now I had been in the Beirut hospital for twelve whole weeks. Little had changed. Nasya had been working with me to restore feeling to my legs so that I could learn to walk again, but we'd made no progress. Still I lay there on my back, helpless. I knew every stain on the ceiling, every crack in the window, and had counted the thirty-two rings that held up the curtain around my bed a thousand times. One, two, three, four... I needed a new distraction to get through the day and maintain my courage. If only I could move!

Suddenly my lungs tightened. I needed fresh air. Looking at the closed curtain, I wished for Pappa's mystical powers so that I could open it with a blink of an eye. No sooner had that passed through my mind than the curtain panels parted and two young girls peeked through, my new pals Evania and her little sister, Gina, whose mother was now sharing the room with me.

"Are you awake?" Evania asked.

"Can we come in?" Gina asked.

I nodded and they tiptoed in.

"Could you please open the curtain?" I asked. Gina smiled and pulled it aside. The metal rings made a small screeching sound against the iron rod. I took a deep breath and filled my lungs with the medicinal smell. An encouraging smile from me brought the girls closer.

"Do you need anything? Water or some juice?"

"Could you please get me some tea?"

They ran over to their mother's bedside and came back to me with a cup of tea, and Gina fed it to me with a spoon.

Evania had helped me write to my parents, and she also brought make-up and used my face for experiments. It brought smiles to the doctors' faces to see what the girls had done to me. We became such close friends that when their mother was discharged from the hospital Evania placed a gold ring with a blue stone on my finger and said, "This will remind you of me, and my promise never to forget you."

I looked at her mother.

"If she wants you to have it, that's fine with me," she said. They had promised to visit me regularly, and they did.

Being paralyzed, I couldn't choose my friends, but I had no problem making them. Older people, men, women, boys, girls—they were all so kind, and I was so grateful to them.

One visitor, however, made me a little uneasy—Kim. He was very sweet, and that was the problem. I wasn't sure how to interpret his kindness or respond to it. The nurse said that he had been visiting me from the very beginning. He must have been in his mid-twenties, slender and tall with a beard and dirty blonde hair. He brought me flowers and a sandwich every day—pita bread rolled up with garlic chicken inside. It tasted so much better than the hospital food, just thinking about it made my mouth water. He read funny stories to make me laugh, and sometimes he would just sit by my bed and watch me sleep. The amount of time he spent at my bedside was a little excessive, but I didn't have the heart to tell him. At the same time, I did nothing to encourage him.

One day Marcia, Mr. Zain's secretary, visited me.

"You've put on weight. What are they feeding you?" she asked when she saw me. It must be Kim's sandwich, I thought, happy with her comment. In Sri Lanka, gaining weight was a sign of wealth and health.

She handed me more letters from my parents, which I tucked under my pillow to read later.

"Seems like you're getting better," Marcia said. I smiled. "You're going to be discharged in two weeks."

"What? I haven't recovered yet!"

"Lisha called Mr. Zain. She has threatened to bomb the hospital if we keep you here any longer."

Bomb the hospital! I tried to say, but the words stuck in my throat. I stared at Marcia. She was perfectly serious. Feeling as if someone had sucked the blood out of my body, I started to sweat.

"Why should it matter to her how long I stay in the hospital?"

"Well, she's the one who pays your hospital bill."

"Lisha is paying my hospital bill?" I asked, astonished.

"Yes, you were under her care at the time of your accident so she is responsible for you."

It felt good knowing that Lisha was paying a price for what she had done to me. Still, her threat hung over me.

"Can she really bomb the hospital?" I asked doubtfully. Lisha was a mystery to me. During the whole time I lived with her I had never seen her husband—if she even had one. I didn't know who she was or what she did for a living. All I knew was that Lisha was rich and powerful.

"There's no telling what she can do. We can't take any chances." Marcia shrugged. "We're making arrangements to send you home as soon as you're released from the hospital, so don't worry."

Too confused to be relieved, I felt sick to my stomach. What if Lisha came and killed me right here in my bed? The thought terrified me.

After Marcia left, I grew panicky. Each time somebody walked into my room I thought it was Lisha. Seeking comfort, I took the letters from under the pillow.

"I cannot tell you how glad I am to hear from you after all this time," Amma wrote, "but to hear that you are in the hospital scares me. What happened? Are you hurt? I can't rest until I see you again. Please come home. I will go to the agency and talk to Barla. I'll find a way to pay them back the money to cancel your contract. I'll beg him to bring you back home."

How did I ever doubt your love, Amma? I thought.

"Your son needs you," the letter went on. "He listens to your tape every day, waves his hands whenever he sees an airplane and calls out to you."

I pressed the letter against my chest, wondering how I would ever tell her what had happened to me. How could I go back to my parents an invalid, and what good would I be to Samadha like this? I felt defeated. Blindly, I had hoped to be walking when I returned, but Lisha's threat had left me no time to recover.

As I was stuffing the letter back under my pillow, Dr. Marwan popped in. "Hello! What happened to that beautiful smile?" He paused. "I have good news for you."

I forced a smile for him but couldn't think of anything nice to say.

"You seem to be doing well, the incision is healing well. There's nothing else we can do for you here. We're going to release you in two weeks." He waited for my response, and when there was none, he continued. "Where are you going to stay until the agency sends you home? You'll need full-time attention. Do you think you can go back with Madame Lisha?"

"No!" I cried. "I'm going back to the agency! Mr. Zain will arrange for—for the care I need," stumbling over my words. Why was this happening to me? Cursing my lifeless legs, I tried to move but failed.

After Dr. Marwan left I called for the nurse and asked to see my physiotherapist, Nasya, the only person I could trust. As I waited for her I pondered my predicament, and by the time Nasya finally arrived, late that afternoon, I was a nervous wreck. The moment her face appeared, I burst out crying.

"What's wrong, child?"

I told her about everything: Lisha's threat, my release in two weeks, the possibility that I might have to move back with Lisha.

Nasya closed her eyes, perturbed. When I was finished she sat down beside me, ran her fingers through my hair and took my hand in hers.

"Don't worry, my dear, I won't let you go back to her. I'll call Mr. Zain, and if he can't provide the care you need, I'll take you in until you're ready to go home. And I'll talk to the doctor." She sounded very confident.

"Can you really do that, will they let you?" I asked pleadingly.

"Yes, I can and I will, trust me. I won't let anything happen to you again."

I looked into Nasya's eyes, grateful for her utter selflessness. But I was still stiff with terror.

"Why don't you talk to the police about this woman?" Nasya asked.

"No, I don't want any more trouble. It would be my word against hers. I can't fight her. I just want to go home."

"Well then, don't worry about her. I'll take care of everything. Trust me."

I tried to convince myself that everything was going to work out, but my helpless body was hard to ignore.

"I'm sorry I failed you, Nasya" I said.

She stood and faced me, her warm smile gone. "I won't let you give up that easily. The time has come to force your courage, to challenge your fate." She looked deep into my eyes. "I've been working on your legs for twelve weeks. If you believe you're going to walk, now is the time to prove it."

She went to the foot of my bed and raised my left leg, letting it rest on her palm and feeling it with her fingers.

"It's now or never. Give me a sign, show me a movement," she begged. I tried but didn't feel a thing.

"Think of your son. Find the strength, find your courage and try to move," she demanded, running her fingers up and down my leg. No feeling. Then she lifted my right leg and ran her fingers over it. "We have only two weeks, help me."

Eyes closed, I tried to visualize each muscle in my legs, tried to feel the touch of Nasya's fingers, tried to move. I imagined myself walking through the front door of my parents' house, Amma running to me and laughing with joy, Pappa hugging me, whispering in my ear, "Take my strength, don't be scared, you can do it," Samadha standing beside me crying, "Ammy, do you love me?" In my mind I took him in my arms and said, "I love you with all the strength in my body!"

All of a sudden Nasya screamed. I opened my eyes. She had her fingers pressed against my ankle and she was smiling, tears running down her cheeks.

"I felt a movement right here!"

"You did?"

"Try to do it again, whatever you did, try it again!"

Tightening every muscle I imagined there was in my body, I tried to move my toes. Sensing the movement again, Nasya bent over and kissed my foot.

"You did it, my child, you did it!"

"But I didn't feel anything. What does it mean?"

"What does this mean? Oh, Ranga, this means there is hope for you now! You won't be bedridden forever. You'll be able to move around when your muscles get stronger. Even though you don't feel anything, your nerves have started to communicate with your brain. All you have to do is to work on them until they are strong enough to help you walk again."

"Really?" I asked excitedly. "Are you sure about this?"

"I *know* you can do it." She came and rested her cheek against mine. I felt like a bird with new wings flying up in the sky, peaceful, free and clear of everything. Thank you, Lord, for giving me hope, I prayed. Thank you for Nasya.

"I'm going to walk again, I'm going to walk again!" I shouted at the top of my lungs.

"You will, my dear, you will. Doctors can't be right all the time, and you can prove them wrong," Nasya said.

I couldn't have asked for anything more. Just the slightest hope of a chance to walk again thrilled me.

That afternoon and into the evening, Nasya worked on my legs. With their muscles paralyzed, my feet had been flopped over for months. Nasya bent them to their natural position and placed a pillow between my soles and the bed railing to keep them from flopping back down.

"Keep moving those muscles and keep the nerves busy," she said. "You won't feel anything, but believe me, you *are* working those muscles. And take short breaks in between." With that, she kissed my cheeks and left.

Stimulated by my triumph, I spent every second trying to move my feet with their long toenails, their wrinkled and peeling skin, urging my cells to get back to work. I felt more courageous than ever.

Later that night Nasya came back to see me, after changing from her white uniform into a pretty red dress. "I just came to tell you that you don't have to be afraid anymore. I've talked to Mr. Zain and the doctors. The hospital staff isn't going to release you to anyone but Mr. Zain. He's making all the arrangements to send you home as soon as you're released. Does that make you happy?"

"Yes," I said, holding both her hands and thanking her.

"Keep working your muscles. I'll see you tomorrow."

I slept peacefully that night, knowing I would be safe from Lisha. Still, in the back of my mind was another worry: What would happen if I wasn't able to stand when I left the hospital? Two weeks was not a long time.

Dr. Assad visited me early the next morning, looking pleased. "You're a strong woman, Miss Suriya," he said. I didn't have to answer him. My smile told him how happy his words made me. "I'll help you any way I can, but remember it's going to take years before you walk on your own. You'll have to work hard to get your nerves to do their job, and there's no guarantee how far you'll progress. So far, we have hope on your right leg, but the left has not shown any sign of recovery. The important thing is not to give up."

"I'll do whatever it takes, I won't give up," I said.

"I'm going to put a cast on you from your neck down to your hip. That will support your spine when you start to move around. You should wear it for six months so that your spine can get used to your weight."

"Thank you for all your help, Doctor," I said, and he left the room whistling.

A while later Nasya came to see me. She removed the pillow from between my feet and the bed railing. I watched my feet standing alone without support from the pillow. I held my breath, waiting for them to flop back down, but they didn't.

"You're a courageous woman," Nasya said.

"I'm beginning to believe that."

"We have a lot to do in these two weeks. I need to get you stronger before they release you."

And so the intense therapy began. Nasya came in twice a day and worked on my legs. A rope was hung above my bed. I used the rope to lift my upper body off the bed and to turn from side to side, and used a pillow to support my back. Within a couple of days I was able to lie on either side without any support to my back.

With my arms growing stronger, I could finally feed myself, reach drawers to get things and shut off lights. Slowly, I started to move the toes in my right foot, but my left foot was still totally paralyzed.

A few days after Dr. Assad's visit, I was taken into a room and guided onto a tall stool. My shoulders and head rested on a counter. I had no place to rest my legs and a male nurse was called in to hold on to them. Dr. Marwan wrapped me with bandages from my neck down to my hips and cut a circle right above my belly. Then he applied cold plaster of Paris over the bandage.

The nurse couldn't hold my legs still because of the weight, and each time his hands moved I screamed in pain, fearing damage to my spine. I prayed for the ordeal to be over.

My big day finally arrived. I was going to stand on my own two feet after being bedridden for three months. If I ever wanted Samadha to see me walk again, I would have to get started that day.

It was a special day for the hospital staff as well, since I had grown so close to them. When Nasya arrived my room was crowded with friends and nurses, all wanting to see me stand on my feet.

"I brought you these so you don't have to wear hospital slippers," Nasya said, handing me a pair of brown-leather butterfly-shaped slippers, along with a soft robe to wear over my hospital gown.

At last, the time had come. Nasya and Nurse Silvia came up to my bed.

"Hold on to the rope and pull yourself up. Don't be scared, I won't let you fall," said Nasya.

I grabbed the rope handle and turned to the right; Nasya put both of her arms under mine and pulled me up to a sitting position. Nurse Sylvia moved my legs off the bed. I felt dizzy for a second and leaned on my helpers. With my arms around their shoulders, I sat on the bed for a few minutes and looked around—at all the smiling faces, some with tears in their eyes. I smiled back at them. The bed in which I had lain for the last three months was covered with flakes of peeled skin.

"How do you feel?" Nasya asked.

"Fine."

"If you aren't dizzy, you can try to stand."

"Yes, I want to."

"Put your weight on us, and first put your right foot on the floor and then the left. But try not to put much weight on the left. Are you ready?"

"Yes."

Nasya put the butterfly slippers on my feet. "Let's do it!"

I stepped onto the floor with the right foot first and then the left. My left leg had no strength and felt lifeless. The knee buckled and, as I slipped, Sylvia pulled me up and supported me. But my right foot stood strong, bearing my weight. "Yea!" I called out joyfully, as the assembled group clapped.

"Put your weight on us and try to take a step," Nasya said. It wasn't easy. I lifted my right foot and took a step, then dragged my left leg behind. It buckled again, but Nasya held me tight.

Those few small steps zapped me of all my strength. I started to shake and was helped back onto the bed, exhausted but thrilled by the prospect of independence.

The next day Nasya brought a wheelchair and took me to the physical therapy department. She put me on a bicycle. At first my feet were attached to automatic pedals, but in a couple of days I was able to pedal myself, and soon I built enough strength to hold on to a railing and take some steps on my own.

While the left leg still showed no sign of recovery, my upper body grew stronger by the day. No longer confined to bed, each day I took a few steps with the help of a nurse. I couldn't stay on my feet for long, two to three minutes at most, but at least now I could tend to some of my needs, brushing my hair, washing myself and writing letters.

As the discharge date approached, my uncertainty grew. I trusted Nasya with my life and believed her promise that I wouldn't be released to Lisha, but I had no guarantee that Mr. Zain would keep his word.

Chapter 11

At the end of two weeks of therapy, by which time I'd regained much more strength in my upper body and had slight movement in the right leg, Dr. Marwan signed my release papers and handed me my medical records.

"I wish you all the best, Ranga," he said. "Please write to me if you have any questions."

"Am I really going to walk without help?" I asked. "Will I recover completely?"

"You've broken the barrier. The rest is up to you." He paused. "Remember, you need to wear the cast for six months, until your spine heals. Don't have the rods in your spine removed at least for the next six months. My suggestion is don't ever take them out unless they start to bother you."

It wasn't the hoped-for answer, but I told myself not to give up, I would do whatever it took to walk again and have my life back. I heard Marcia's voice at the reception area. Thank you, Lord, for not sending me back to Lisha, I prayed.

I said goodbye to all my friends at the hospital. Nasya hugged me. "When the cast comes off in six months, maybe I can visit you in Sri Lanka and help you with the physical therapy."

"Would you really?" I asked her doubtfully.

"If I survive this war, I'll certainly try," she said, hugging me.

"God will protect you," I told her.

It was like leaving home, departing the hospital that had sheltered me and given me so many friends, and as Nurse Enid wheeled me out and laid me down on the back seat of Marcia's car, I was overcome with melancholy.

Marcia drove me to the hotel to meet with Mr. Zain. A steward from the restaurant came and helped me inside, the same young man with the birthmark on his cheek who had smiled at me after my arrival in Lebanon. His brown eyes widened when he recognized me. He looked handsome in his steward uniform—black pants, white shirt, red vest buttoned at the waist. After taking a few steps in the red carpeted corridor leading toward the elevator, I started to hurt.

"I have to rest," I said, and the steward led me into the restaurant where I sat down at a table, shaking and sweating. The restaurant looked the same except for the centerpiece—the single roses had been replaced with round vases of small plants.

"I'll be right back," Marcia said and ran up to Mr. Zain's office.

I nodded and tried to lean back on the chair. The black wooden seat felt cold and rigid beneath me, and the smell of food made my stomach growl.

"We heard what happened to you, but Marcia said we couldn't visit you at the hospital," the steward said.

"That's all right, I'm here now."

"My name is Sarath," he said. He looked very young, maybe about eighteen. His childish smile was charming, his voice gentle.

"I'm Ranga," I said, looking into his eyes.

"Did you have your lunch yet?" he asked

"No, I didn't even have time to eat my breakfast," I said.

He smiled. "Let me get you some lunch." He disappeared through the swinging doors into the kitchen, then Marcia returned and asked me to come upstairs to meet with Mr. Zain. Hanging on to her hand, I stood up.

"I ordered some lunch for her, it will only take a few minutes," Sarath called, coming back out of the kitchen.

"Oh! Thank you, Sarath, but Mr. Zain needs to see her right away. I'll make sure she gets lunch."

Sarath looked at me with concern as I dragged myself over to the lift with Marcia's help.

As we entered the agency, Mr. Zain came out of his office wearing his usual smile. "Welcome back, Miss Suriya. Look at you, you're walking!"

I looked at him in disbelief. This is what you call walking? I thought, trying to take another step toward the chair in the reception area. Seeing my struggle, Mr. Zain rushed forward and helped Marcia get me to the chair. Guilt was written all over his face; he tried to cover it with a smile and I felt almost sorry for him. After all, he had kept his word and here I was in his care instead of Lisha's. At least I had to thank him for that. So I looked up and smiled at him. He ran his fingers nervously over his red tie. When I first arrived in Lebanon, he had intimidated me. Not any more; nothing could destroy my new-found courage or my self-esteem.

Marcia went back to her reception desk, took out a small mirror and freshened her lipstick. The telephone rang and rang. At last she answered it. "Employment agency, Marcia speaking," she said, tapping her long red fingernails on the glass table as she listened.

"I would like a written statement from you explaining what happened, how you fell off the balcony," Mr. Zain said, and paused. When I didn't respond he went on, "Did you say you felt dizzy and fell, or did Lisha push you off the balcony?"

I looked straight into his eyes. "You didn't believe me before?"

He seemed startled, and at a loss for words. Secretly I enjoyed his loss of composure. He exchanged glances with Marcia.

"Get her to sign those papers and take her to the hotel," he said, and turned to me. "You need to sign some papers in order for us to help you with your recovery. We will pay all your expenses until you fully recover."

"That would be nice," I said, trying to believe him. He nodded and retreated into his office.

Marcia brought me a stack of papers. I had no energy to read through all that material, so I just signed them, and after taking them back, Marcia finished up her work.

"I need to lie down," I said. Marcia looked at me and must have recognized the pain I was in; she pulled three chairs together and helped me lie down.

"I'll take you to your room quickly," she said, and disappeared into Mr. Zain's office for a half hour.

Then she drove me to another hotel not far from the agency. Two bellboys at the door came to help me out of the car and into the lounge. I sat down on a velvet-cushioned couch while Marcia hurried to the reception desk. It didn't strike me as a well-maintained hotel; the greenish walls needed new paint, the brown carpeted floor shampooing. There were three couches in the lounge and a small round table in the middle with two ashtrays and a few Lebanese magazines. The middle-aged man at the reception desk looked drained. Soft background music was playing my favorite song, "*Rain and Tears*."

Marcia came back with the keys and took me upstairs to my room. A large suite with two bedrooms, it had soft pink walls and there were pink sheets on the bed. The bedding was damp, and the musty air made me sneeze. I pinched my nose to stop from sneezing. It hurt terribly along my incision whenever I had to sneeze or cough.

"Well then, see you later," said Marcia.

"I'm so hungry, will someone bring me food?" I asked

She turned around, hand on the doorknob. "I'll ask at the reception desk if they can bring you some food."

"Who is going to help me with my needs?" I asked.

She was out the door now. "I'll arrange that too." She closed the door behind her, leaving me alone in the room. Exhausted, I fell asleep within minutes, dreaming of the chicken sandwich Kim had brought to the hospital every day.

The sound of the phone woke me. It was dark, and I reached out to the nightstand and switched on the light. I couldn't answer the phone because it was in the other room. The clock said nine P.M. My stomach growled and my bladder was full. If only I could use the bathroom, I thought, I could go back to sleep and forget my hunger until the morning. I tried to get off the bed, but without a railing I couldn't do it on my own.

While I worried about wetting the bed, the doorknob turned and a man walked into the room.

He was short and middle-aged, with a yellow shirt opened at the neck and a loosened tie. His bald head shone under the overhead light.

"I was just passing by and thought I'd come in and say hello," he said, approaching me with a grin. My chest tightened as he sat down beside me, resting his hand on the breast area of my cast, which was hidden under the sheets.

"I'm paralyzed, I'm wearing a cast," I said quickly, hoping to elicit his sympathy.

Feeling the hard cast under his palm, he jumped off the bed and moved away from me, face turning red. He stared at me with pity

"I'm so sorry, I had no idea you were a serious patient. I just came to check on you to see if everything was all right."

"Who are you? Did Marcia send you to help me?" I asked.

"I'm the hotel manager. Mr. Zain didn't say anything about you when he booked this room. I'm very sorry if I scared you, please tell me if there's anything I can do to help."

Relieved, I seized the opportunity. "I really need to use the bathroom, but I cannot get off the bed by myself. Marcia promised to send help and food, but no one came. I haven't eaten all day. Do you think you can send someone to help me before I wet the bed?"

"This time of the night I won't be able to find you any help," he said, his voice breaking. "I'm afraid you have no choice but to use my help. As for food, the kitchen is closed now so I can't get you a real meal, but I'll find you something."

I thanked God for sending him to my room, even if he had had bad thoughts in his mind. He helped me off the bed, walked me into the bathroom, turned around and waited as I emptied my bladder. Then he suggested that I take the other bed, which was close to the phone. I agreed and he helped me settle back down, moving the table close so I could reach the phone.

"You can only call the reception desk—you can't call anyone outside."

"What is the use of a phone if I can't call anyone?"

"You can receive incoming calls," he said, and left the room to fetch me some food. A few minutes later he was back with crackers and a pot of tea. I ate a couple of crackers while he waited, and he helped me with the tea. After I was all settled in my bed, he left the room, promising to send me help the next day, and I went back to sleep peacefully.

I woke up as usual, early in the morning, and praised the Lord while waiting for help. Finally I called the reception desk to order breakfast. The hotel manager sent a room maid to help me, a young Lebanese woman who only spoke Arabic. I used hand signals and a few halting Arabic words to tell her what I needed. She was very gentle with me.

No one from the agency visited or called. I wanted to call Nasya and tell her what was happening, and when the manager dropped by to visit me that morning, I gave him her telephone number to call. Time was of the essence. All hope of regaining my strength depended on continued physical therapy. Without help, I would remain bedridden and lose all the progress I'd made.

As I lay there waiting to hear from Marcia, Sarath came for a visit.

"How did you know where I was?" I asked him, surprised.

"I have my ways," he said proudly. "So tell me, how are you feeling? Did Marcia give you any food yesterday?"

I told him everything that had happened. He was furious at Marcia, and the manager's behavior didn't surprise him.

"I've heard about him from other girls who were here. He tries the same thing with all of them, but I didn't think he'd try it with you."

"He didn't know I was paralyzed."

"He's a nice guy, but a womanizer," Sarath said, glancing around the room. He went over to the windows, which were shattered from explosions, and opened the curtain and the shutters. Cool fresh air with a slight scent of rain rushed into the room. Sarath smiled and pulled a chair close to the bed.

"I wanted to come yesterday, but I had to cover the night shift and couldn't get away."

"It's all right," I said, wishing he had come.

"I'm going to visit you every day, and help you anyway I can until they send you home."

I was glad to hear that, and thanked him for being so caring. He went out and brought lunch for both of us. While we were eating, Marcia showed up.

"Aren't you lucky, my dear, to make friends so quickly," she said significantly.

"You promised to send me food and help yesterday, but no one came. What happened?" I asked, ignoring her comment.

"Well, I couldn't find anyone yesterday, that's why I'm here now."

It was no use being mad at her. Needing her help until they sent me back, I had to be patient. Instead of complaining about what had happened the day before, I requested her help in the days to come.

"I can't find anyone to spend the whole day with you," she said. "The housekeeping staff here will help you during the day, but that's all I can do."

"Fine," I said. It was better than nothing.

She promised to check on me the next day and left.

"I'll drop in every day to make sure you're okay," Sarath said. "Don't worry, I'll help you even if she doesn't send anyone."

With his help, I got out of bed and took a few steps over to the window. Shops and restaurants lined both sides of the street below, which was busy with pedestrians.

"Were there any bombs dropped around here?" I asked.

"Some time back yes, but not anymore. Don't worry, this place is safe. Sometimes you can hear the sound of explosions but they're far away. You'll be safe here, I promise."

Sarath was a saint. He spent the entire afternoon with me before leaving for his night shift, then called me from work to make sure I was okay. In the ensuing days, the maids helped me when they came to clean the room, but it was Sarath who really tended to my needs. He made sure I got all my meals, helped me with my exercises and checked on me before I went to sleep.

The days dragged on and my patience was wearing thin. It was my second week at the hotel. A constant rain made the room cold and wet. The roof started to leak and water blew into the room through the broken windows. I had no clothes other than the gown Nasya had given me the day I left the hospital and a couple of hospital gowns. When I asked for my suitcase, Marcia said that Lisha had not returned it to them. She promised to get it before I left the country. Is Mr. Zain going to pay me for the months I worked for Lisha and Beth? I wondered, and decided to ask about that when I talked to Marcia next time.

After a long couple of weeks, the agonizing stay at the hotel was finally over—I was going home! The rain had stopped and sunlight streamed through the window. It was a fine morning. Only a few more hours, I told myself joyfully. Sarath had come to help me get ready for my journey. He went to the store and bought me something to wear—a long orange nightgown, pleated at the neck, which covered my ugly cast. Had it not been for Sarath I wouldn't have survived my stay at the hotel, and words couldn't adequately express the depth of my gratitude.

Waiting for Marcia to take me to the airport, I was too nervous to eat. The phone jangled, startling me. Oh, no, I thought, the plans have been changed. With a sickening feeling I picked up the receiver.

"Something's come up, I can't make it," Marcia said. "I'm sending our driver Ahmed to take you to the airport."

"Oh," I sighed. "What about my suitcase?"

"I'm sending it with Ahmed. He'll check it for you. There's another girl traveling with you. She'll help you on your journey."

I hesitated a moment, finding my courage.

"What about my pay? I need the pay for the months I worked."

"Yes, Ahmed will give it to you at the airport," she said. I didn't detect anything unusual in her voice and couldn't tell if she was lying. At the time I didn't have a choice but to take her word for it. She wished me luck.

"Thank you," I said, and really meant it.

There were no bags to pack. The dirty hospital gowns I'd worn for two weeks were thrown away. Dressed in the orange nightgown, I lay on my bed waiting for Ahmed. He was the same driver with girlish face who had brought me from the airport seven months before. With his help and Sarath's I went downstairs, thanked the hotel manager for his help and got into the back seat with the other girl. Looking out the window I reached for Sarath's hand, "I don't know how to thank you for being so kind to me."

"There's no need for thanks Ranga, I am glad I was able to help you. Write to me as soon as you can, so I know you are alright," said Sarath.

"I promise," and let go off his hand and turn to the girl next to me.

"I'm Latha," she said.

"I'm Ranga."

"What happened to you?" she asked.

"Didn't they tell you?"

"Marcia asked me to help you, she said you couldn't walk." Latha studied me for a moment. "Wait a minute—aren't you the person who was pushed off the balcony?"

I didn't feel like talking about it so I just looked out the window.

Latha, a twenty-eight-year-old unmarried woman from Ratnapura, Sri Lanka, was going home after completing her two-year contract as a housemaid. She wore a purple and blue saree, pearl earrings, gold bangles and a heavy gold chain with a cross around her neck. She was tiny, about five feet tall, and I couldn't imagine she'd be much help. I'll find a way somehow, I tried to convince myself.

When we reached the airport, Ahmed helped me out of the car and over to the check-in counter, his free hand carrying my long lost suitcase, which Lisha had returned to the agency. Once the luggage was tagged and I was checked in, he turned to Latha. "Help her get to the plane," he said, then with a glance at me added, "Good luck, have a safe trip," and turned to leave.

I called out to him, "Where's my money? Marcia said she gave it to you."

"What money?" he said. "What are you talking about? She didn't give me any money."

I thought he was feigning surprise. "Well then, could you take me to a phone? I need to call her. I'm not leaving without my money."

He gave me a curious look. "Do you want to miss your flight? You don't have much time. Why do you want to fight over this now when you have the chance to leave?"

He was right—there was no way I was going to miss the flight. But I was angry.

"I'll take my chances," I said firmly. "Will you please take me to a phone?"

Looking scared, he reached for his wallet and took out some money. "I don't want you to miss this plane. I have some money, here take this," he said. I counted three hundred pounds—one and a half month's pay. He owed me for another two months. In the background my flight was being announced. The gate was open and people were starting to board. I had to hurry—it was a long walk to the gate, and I needed all the time I could get.

"It is not right to steal from me," I said. "You should be ashamed of yourself if you have!"

"I promise you they didn't give me any money," he insisted, but I didn't believe him.

It was not worth it to miss my plane for a few hundred pounds, so I accepted the money.

I turned to Latha and, holding on to her shoulders, started to walk. She was carrying two handbags, and it was difficult for her to support me and juggle these at the same time. Having already pushed myself to the limit, I asked Latha to take me to a bench so I could sit down and catch my breath. Ahead of us loomed the long corridor. Clearly, Latha wouldn't be able to get me to the plane in time, and so I started calling out for help from passengers rushing by. Some just walked away without even looking back, but one gentleman stopped in front of me. He was old, his navy blue buttoned-up shirt had no room to breathe on his tight belly and a brown belt held his gray pants in place. He carried a briefcase in his hand.

"You need help?" he asked, raising his eyebrows.

"Please, sir, I can't walk on my own, and my friend can't help me. Could you please help me get to the plane?"

"Yes, of course! What's wrong with you?" he asked.

"I'm just out of the hospital after major surgery," I lied, fearing he wouldn't help me if he knew the truth. "I can't walk by myself yet."

He handed his briefcase to Latha and I leaned on his strong hairy arms, hung onto his shoulders and started to walk. My left leg buckled, but he held onto me tightly.

"You should have talked to the airline personnel when you checked in. They would have given you a wheelchair or carried you to the plane."

"Really? Why didn't anyone tell me that?" I was in such agony that I didn't hear his answer. My legs and back hurt terribly. By the time we were outside the terminal, heading toward the stairs to board the plane, my legs collapsed and I slipped. The gentlemen grabbed me and picked me up in his arms. From the top of the stairs the stewardess saw what was happening and came running to us.

"Are you okay, madam? Do you need help?"

"Yes, please, I can't walk anymore," I said, wiping my tears. She called for help, and as I thanked the kind gentleman, two flight attendants came up to carry me into the plane. The two attendants took me to my seat.

"What's wrong? Why are you crying?" they asked.

"Was I booked like a regular passenger? I'm in pain, I need to lie down," I said, opening my handbag and producing the medical report.

"Oh my God!" one of the stewardesses said. "How could anyone do this? Whoever booked you on this plane should have reserved three seats for you."

They carried me to first class, laid me down across three seats with plenty of pillows and blankets, and kept a close eye on me during the flight. Despite the pain and exhaustion, I was grateful for all this tender care from strangers, and grateful that the plane hadn't been fully booked.

I had to change flights in Dubai. When we reached the airport there, the stewardesses carried me out of the airplane and into a medical room where they let me rest while I waited for the next flight. A nurse massaged my legs and arms and gave me painkillers. The room was quiet and I didn't see anyone around. I was afraid to close my eyes, thinking that I might fall asleep and they would forget to take me to the plane. When I couldn't stand it any longer I asked the nurse if they would let Latha stay with me until people boarded the plane, and she said yes.

This time it was an Air Lanka flight, with a Sri Lankan crew. Before takeoff the pilot came to talk to me.

"If you need anything, just ask and my crew will keep you safe," he said.

"I know I'm safe now," I said gratefully, hugely relieved to be around Sri Lankans again. The flight attendants had their hair tied up and wore *kandyan,* similar to saris, made of green fabric with a border of peacock feathers at the hemline. Two flight attendants stayed by my side throughout the flight. When the plane bounced from turbulence, they held me close and talked to distract me from the agony. Their jokes made me laugh and they showered me with food and drinks and small gifts—cards, pens and a calculator.

Just before landing, the pilot called the Katunayake airport and asked them to have a stretcher ready. At last, after seven grueling months, I'm home! I thought when the wheels hit the runway with a thud.

The flight attendants lifted me onto the stretcher, wheeled me into the airport and cleared me through customs. After retrieving my luggage, they shifted me into a wheelchair and took me to the arrival area where my parents would be waiting. I breathed deeply, relishing the sticky, salty air, and let out a long sigh. A weight had been lifted and my heart was light.

It was around two in the morning. Eagerly my eyes searched the crowd, one face after another. Please, please, where are you, Amma? I thought. Gradually, all the hope that had built up for a cheerful reunion dissipated, like air leaking from a balloon, and I grew alarmed.

"Do you see anyone?" the flight attendant said, wheeling me through the crowd. Maybe they weren't informed of my arrival, I thought. "No, they're not here," I said. "How am I going to get home now?"

He looked around again, thinking. "Don't worry, we can take you home. Let me talk to my supervisor." He wheeled me back to the counter and I waited while they made the arrangements.

I was laid in an airline bus and three airline officers accompanied me home, all young men in white uniforms. Latha, who still had a long journey home, decided to come along with us; she could spend the night at my parents' house, which was on the way, and catch a bus in the morning.

During my time in Lebanon my parents had sold the farm and moved into a rented house in my mother's hometown of Chilaw. By the time we got there, it was around four in the morning. The whole town seemed to be asleep; the only sound I heard was the barking of street dogs.

Finally, I thought, everything's going to get better.

The bus came to a halt and I was surprised to see the lights on in my parents' house. What are they doing up so early? I wondered. One of the officers knocked on the door while another helped me off the bus and walked me to the house.

Pappa came to the door. "Chuty Duwa!" he said, shocked. Taking me in his arms, he shouted for my mother. I saw Amma peering through the curtain. "Who is that?" she said, and then seeing me she screamed and ran over. "You came home! Thank you, God, thank you, God, for answering my prayers!" she cried, tears pouring down her cheeks.

After I was put on the bed to rest, my parents thanked the officers and served them tea.

"No one told us you were coming!" Amma said. "We didn't hear anything from the agency. We were getting ready to go and talk to the Minister of Parliament to ask his help."

"Where's Samadha?"

"He's still asleep. I'll go get him."

Amma went to her room, woke up my son and put him next to me. I hugged him as best I could and kissed his sleepy face. Suddenly he grabbed my handbag, which was on the side of the bed, and rifled through it. "Where's the money, Ammy?"

Samadha had remembered my promise—that I was going to make money and give him a better life. Everyone laughed, but I felt sad. "When I'm all better I'll find a way to make money," I said, not wanting to disappoint him.

After the airline officers left, Pappa and Amma sat down and peppered me with questions about what had happened. Although, in deciding to jump for my life, I hadn't chosen to die—in fact, I was hoping to live—I didn't want my parents to get the impression that I had tried to commit suicide and that I had been willing to leave my son behind. And so I told them everything except for the part about jumping off the balcony. "I don't remember how I fell," I said.

After hearing my story, Pappa said that we should file a case against the agency. Samadha wrapped his arms around me and said, "I don't need any money, Ammy. Please don't go back." His innocent eyes filled with tears as he kissed me. I kissed him back and promised never to leave him again.

I handed my medical records to Pappa and he looked over my X-rays.

"We should find an ayurvedic doctor and start you with herbal treatment," he said.

"But the doctors said that the cast should stay on for six months," I said, doubting his opinion.

"That's not going to do you any good. It has to come off before that. The recovery will be much quicker with the herbal medicine," Pappa insisted.

Knowing I couldn't argue with my father, I thought of asking Amma to convince him not to go against the doctor's orders, and decided to write to Dr. Marwan for his advice.

Later that morning Pastor Nayake, from my parents' church, dropped by and was surprised to see me home. After hearing my story, he said I should tell it to the paper to prevent other innocent girls from getting hurt. I told him I didn't like the idea of publishing my story in the paper. Nor did my parents. He left and a couple of hours later came back with a reporter anyway.

Pastor Nayake and the reporter tried to convince my parents to go public with the story, telling Pappa he would have a good case if it got in the paper. My father was determined to fight the agency, and that made him believe the reporter.

I sensed that it was going to be a disaster, but I didn't want to dishonor my parents. God had given me back my life, and I had vowed that if I made it through I would be the best, most obedient child possible. If they wanted to fight it, I had to support them. So I told the reporter what happened in Lebanon, divulging as few details as possible. Latha, however, who was still at my parents' house, gave the reporter a clear picture of a maid's life in Lebanon. She also told him how people believed that Lisha had pushed me off the balcony. They took pictures and I tried to hide my face so no one would recognize me.

After going through so much agony, all I had wanted was to come home and recover. Now I was being pulled into a battle I didn't want. I rifled through my luggage for the diary I had kept at Lisha's, and when I found it my heart sank. All the pages had been ripped out. Without those diary entries—without proof of what had happened to me—I was as defenseless as an oyster without its shell.

Chapter 12

Seeing Samadha's innocent face made me realize how lucky I was to be alive, and more aware than ever of the chance I had taken with my life. Burdened by guilt, I questioned my judgment. *Would* there have been another way out? Lisha could no longer hurt me, but I was left with the doubt of having been wrong. I vowed never to tell the truth to another living soul—to let everyone believe that Lisha had pushed me.

Sitting beside me on the bed, Samadha listened to my made-up stories and sang and played games with me. Some days he fell asleep next to me and I watched him smiling in his dreams. His delicate heart had been scarred; I had to mend it with my love while healing my own soul.

My guilt was compounded as I lay in bed all day watching Amma working to help me mend. Thrilled to have me back, she tended to me with loving patience, never complaining. "In my dreams," she said, "I saw you walking. I made a promise to God that if He sent you back to me, I would take you to church to be a witness for Him."

I wanted to tell her the truth, to explain how God had shown me a miracle, but I had disappointed her too many times and didn't think she would understand. So I held back my thoughts, burying the truth even deeper.

Amma's burden was made worse by the house she and Pappa were renting. It was a huge six-bedroom home with a big kitchen and a large living room, surrounded, outside, by guava, banana and papaya trees. The problem was there was no toilet and no running water, just a well and an outhouse in the backyard. Since we were so close to the sea, the outhouse was built above ground to prevent it from flooding.

Since I couldn't climb up and down the stairs to the outhouse, Amma took a chair, cut a hole in the seat and placed a bucket underneath. Each time she emptied that bucket, I was ashamed of myself forever believing she didn't love me. I wanted to hug her and tell her how sorry I was for all the mistakes I'd made, and for all the trouble she'd had to go through. But I lacked the courage. Instead, I suffered inside while she continued to prove just how much she loved me.

Another problem was the soft white sand in the yard, which brought ants and insects into the house. I worried that the ants or bed bugs would get into my cast. My mother placed cans filled with water underneath the bed legs to prevent ants climbing up to the bed.

Sri Lanka's hot climate made the cast even more uncomfortable. My whole body itched, and Amma tried to keep me as cool as possible. She laid me across the bed, placed a basin of water next to the bed and washed my hair, arms and legs. Then she soaked a long bandage in some cologne I had brought home from the hospital. After rolling it lengthwise into a long thin wick, she inserted the bandage through my cast and moved it up and down to relieve the itching. The wet bandage touched the scar on my back like gentle fingertips, softly scratching.

"Oh, that feels so good, Amma. How do you always know what to do?"

"I am your Amma," she said, and in her beautiful soprano voice started to sing a lullaby that she had sung to me as a baby. That was the only song that had calmed me down as a baby, she said. She sang with such emotion that I found myself drifting off to a place where no suffering existed, and fell asleep.

I had become a newborn again in my mother's care, and my body depended on her to rebuild its strength. I didn't enjoy the dependence for a second, and felt unworthy, but it did make me crave to be the best mother to my own child, and the best daughter to my mother. It made me want to make it to the finish line.

In the meantime, the story came out in the newspaper with my picture. The journalist twisted it all around, and it brought bad publicity. People started to talk, misquoting the story and spinning their own versions. Rumors flew all over town. Posters and flyers were distributed to the public, and people from neighboring towns came to gawk.

I hid out in my room, feeling imprisoned. Neighbors paced in front of the house hoping to catch a glimpse of me, and some even peeked through the windows and threw stones at the house. Amma tried to catch them but they ran away laughing.

My poor mother would drag herself back from the shops, her eyes red from crying. She never said anything to me, but one day I overheard her talking with Pappa.

"People are making up filthy stories about her," she told him. "The word on the street is that the crazy woman pushed her off the balcony for having an affair with her husband."

"Who cares what anyone says? Don't worry about it," said Pappa.

"It's easy for you to say, but think about her. How is she ever going to have a respectable life in this town? They say she deserved what happened to her, and they're cursing us for taking her back. They think she worked as a prostitute in Lebanon."

Why, why? my heart screamed. I turned over on my bed, facing the wall, pretending to sleep while my angry tears soaked into the pillow. How was I ever going to make things right?

It was hard to live with shame and maintain my dignity in the community. I tried to tell my friends and relatives what had really happened in Lebanon, but no matter what I said, they washed their hands of me.

Only my parents believed me. "Why do you care what other people say or think about you? You know what you are inside your heart. Do whatever you think is right, and don't worry about the world," was Pappa's advice. Those words were precious to me; they strengthened my soul as I struggled to start a new life with my son.

One afternoon I was surprised to see my long-lost husband at our doorstep. It had been two years since we'd seen each other and we were still married. I was lying on the sofa in the living room reading a book. He just stood in front of me silently, looking pale, thinner and old—the handsome man I had married was gone. His eyes were sympathetic, and he looked at me as if in apology. My eyes welled up with tears as I watched him leave. He went onto the verandah with our son. Samadha was thrilled to see his father and enjoyed every second with him. I listened to their laughter and grieved over not being able to fill that empty space in my child's life.

Samadha didn't understand why his father never visited him and why we couldn't go back to live with him, but he never questioned me. I asked Tilak if he could visit Samadha more often and he smiled, nodded and walked away.

I never received any money from the agency for my medical expenses, as Mr. Zain had promised. My parents tried their best to fight for a settlement, but the Sri Lankan government left us to wage our own battle. I had allowed my face to be plastered all over the country and had lived with obscene accusations—all for nothing. I had believed I would win the battle in the end, but without my diary, we had only my words and they were not enough.

I had no way of getting back at Mr. Zain—worse, no way of punishing Lisha.

My heart was filled with rage and hatred, and the only good it did was to make me stronger. I tried to sit longer and to walk more often, even when it hurt. The best way to face the world, I decided, was to be a winner. With that determination, I forced myself to bury the past.

Sarath wrote to me often. I never heard from Nasya, or the two girls Evania and Gina, and I worried about them getting hurt in the escalating war in Beirut. Dr. Marwan, however, responded to my letter immediately. He confirmed that the cast should remain for six months and the rods at least a year. Yet Pappa insisted that I get the herbal treatment. I stayed in the cast for three months, then finally agreed with Pappa to have it removed and follow an herbal regimen. He found a famous ayurvedic practitioner, Veda Nandasena, who cut off the cast, applied oil over my body, covered me with a paste made from herbs and wrapped me with bandages. The paste and the oil were sticky and had a bad odor. The good part, though, was that I could take regular showers whenever the paste was changed. I endured Dr. Nandasena's treatment only to satisfy my parents. In my heart, I knew there was nothing anyone could do to speed up the recovery. It was simply a matter of time, determination, and faith in myself. In the long run having the cast removed early didn't make a difference.

The skin on both legs remained numb. Then one day I felt an itch in my left leg and instinctively, my hand reached down and scratched. There was a red spot; a bug had bitten me. Digging my fingernails into the skin, I scratched as hard as I could, but it was no use—it felt as if I was scratching a log. The skin was numb and yet still I sensed the itch. It was a good sign.

Then some sensation returned to the right leg and with excitement I kept touching every inch of my leg to believe I wasn't dreaming. Pappa was convinced it was the herbal medicine that brought the sensation to my leg and I let him enjoy his triumph.

It was about six months before I could take a step or two without help, leaning against a wall for support. My shoulders weren't even—the left was higher than the right—and I tried to correct my posture as I dragged myself forward, Samadha by my side, guiding me. He laughed and hugged me when I failed, but I was determined. As my body grew stronger, so did my will.

Once again, help came from an unexpected source. Pappa had a close friend, Dr. Sarasinghe, a wealthy dentist from Negombo, Pappa's hometown and the place I had last attended school. Dr. Sarasinghe came to visit me every week with his kindly wife. Pappa had given her some psychological counseling and, feeling indebted to him, they wanted to return the favor. To give me a new start they offered us one of their houses in Negombo rent free. At first my parents refused, but several months of pressure from Dr. and Mrs. Sarasinghe finally broke through this resistance.

It was a modern five-bedroom home with an American-style garage surrounded by a six-foot wall. The large foyer, its red-cement floor polished to a shine, was part porch, part living room and dining area. Best of all, the house had a bathroom with running water.

It was the perfect place for us. Pappa could now run his clinic out of home, Amma's duties were considerably lightened with the access to running water, and I could sit in the front without worrying about the neighbors. Mrs. Sarasinghe, who lived next door, often dropped by to chat and keep me company. Other than my relatives and close friends, no one knew who I was or where I came from. The privacy was blissful.

I hid my past in the new house, tried not to think or talk about it. For me, the girl Ranga had died with the fall and been buried in Lebanon. I was a different person now, and to mark the change I took to using my middle name, Trish.

My strength continued to grow, and eventually Amma was accompanying me for short walks around the neighborhood. One Saturday, which happened to be my birthday, my parents were in church and I decided to surprise Amma by walking there on my own. Though my name had long since been dropped from the church's roster for marrying a Buddhist, I still went to church whenever my heart desired. The Adventist church was right behind our house, not too far away. I walked through the doors and sat next to Amma, who kissed me and smiled as we stood up to pray. Scanning the congregation, I recognized some of the church members but no one stared at me and I felt at ease.

Then the pastor's voice said, "Please sit down," and my chest tightened. I glanced up at the pulpit and there he was, Geoffrey, my first love, standing up there with his sweet smile.

"Please remember my wife in your prayers," he said to the congregation. "She's in the hospital waiting to deliver our baby."

It was the first time I had seen him since the breakup; so much had happened since then and no one had mentioned his name in front of me so I had no idea what had become of him. And there he was, standing in front of me as a pastor, a married man and a soon-to-be-father. *Wife! My wife!* His words rang in my head.

I felt worthless, ashamed of myself, living with my parents and hiding my past. Suspecting that he didn't notice me, I stole another glance at him. He looked the same, just a little taller and slimmer. He announced that he was going to be the church's pastor for the coming year. When the congregation stood up to sing, I sneaked out of the church and hobbled home. Suddenly all the strength I had gained through my long recovery seemed like a lie.

Mrs. Sarasinghe had invited all the church members to a birthday party for me that evening, and despite the contretemps earlier that day I had to attend. I did my best to avoid Geoffrey but right before he left, he came looking for me. In front of all the guests he said, "Happy birthday" and reached out to shake my hand. Feeling a sudden urge to embarrass him, I simply turned around and walked away.

Mrs. Sarasinghe came up to me afterwards. "Geoffrey was shocked at what you did, but I think it served him right for the way he hurt you."

It didn't give me any satisfaction and I was sorry for insulting him in front of his congregation, but I was still angry with him. As the days went by I felt that I had to talk to him if I was ever going to find peace in my heart. I waited for a chance to meet him accidentally, and rehearsed in my head what I would say to him, but it was all a fantasy. The truth is I lacked the courage to face him alone.

Fortunately, as time went on my resentment dwindled and I was able to concentrate on healing myself, spiritually as well as physically.

One year had passed since my fall from Lisha's balcony. My shoulders were even now, if slightly hunched, and I walked without a limp. Sensation had returned to the whole right leg and part of my left leg. One day with Amma by my side, I set out for the beach a mile from home. Gazing at strangers to see if anyone noticed me, I realized that in their eyes I was just another pedestrian on the road. My back started to hurt a little but my legs didn't give up and I made it all the way to the shore.

Resting on the golden sand, feeling the cool wind against my skin and listening to the rhythmic sound of waves breaking on the shore, I felt as if I had recovered completely—no, not just recovered, as if I had been reborn. Pain and the endurance it required had molded me into a new person, a woman of once-unimaginable willpower. The time had come to start my life over and support my son.

How to do this was not so clear. Bandula Athukorala, the gentleman from Colombo who had offered help on the plane to Lebanon, came to mind. Although I had turned him down then, I hoped he might help me now. But first I had to find him.

"Amma," I said on our way back home, "I need to make a trip to Colombo." I told her about Bandula, said he was an executive director of some company, that I wanted to ask him for a job and I wanted to go alone. Naturally, Amma was worried about my traveling to the city alone, but I insisted.

I woke up early the next morning and dressed up in a light purple sari with a flowery border, tucked my long hair up high, showing my short neck and the gold earrings on my ears. I wore my mother's high heels to make me tall. For the first time in ages, I looked respectable.

Amma was still pleading to come along, but I didn't give in to her. "Everything's going to be fine," I assured her. She walked me to the Negombo bus station and waited until I got on a bus. Please God, help me find Bandula, I prayed, sitting down in a window seat.

It took almost an hour and a half for the bus to travel the twenty-two miles to Colombo. People, animals and carts choked the narrow road and the vehicle inched forward, dropping people off and gathering others up at each of the numerous stops. The bus was packed and I was glad to have a window seat.

At last the bus came to a halt at the Pettah stop in Colombo, the central hub for buses departing for destinations all across Sri Lanka. I waited in my seat until everyone had piled out, then slowly made my way through the station to find the next bus to Colpetty, where Bandula had told me he worked.

The station was crowded and noisy. Vendors shouted at passersby, competing to sell lottery tickets, drinks, fruit, clothes and shoes, conductors yelled out their announcements, hungry children begged. Standing serenely in the midst of all this deafening turmoil was the Bo tree, considered sacred by most Sri Lankans.

I crossed the road, dodging vendors and beggars, and boarded the bus to Colpetty. On the way there I began daydreaming about the life I would build for Samadha. I would have my own business and it would be hugely successful. We would live in a castle on a hill, surrounded by acres of flowers, herbs and spices and bordered by a natural forest. At the bottom of the hill there would be a lake stocked with silvery fish. The castle would have many floors, and from the third floor a waterfall would cascade down to a pond on the ground floor. The second floor would be filled with toys reserved for all the children in the neighboring villages.

"Next stop Colpetty," the conductor yelled.

With a jolt, I stood up. The bus was packed and I was sitting toward the back. "I'm getting off, I'm getting off!" I cried, hoping the conductor would hear me as I squeezed past the bodies toward the exit. I had come so far, I couldn't take a chance of missing my stop. Standing on the bottom stair of the exit was the conductor, a skinny young fellow with his shirt half buttoned.

"Make room for the lady to get off," he shouted, and thanking him I eased myself down onto the pavement.

I was on Galle Road, the only highway to northern Sri Lanka. A few yards away was the ocean, but the waves couldn't be heard for all the commotion on the sidewalks, which were crawling with merchants and pedestrians. In front of me a woman wearing rags that looked as if they had never been washed suckled a naked baby. I put some change in her palm, then, not knowing how to get to Bandula's office, asked a woman next to me for directions to the address on his card. She told me it was around the corner, across from the Liberty Cinema. I thanked her and started walking.

The cool sea breeze carried the smell of food from nearby restaurants. Feeling strong and lighthearted, smiling at everyone who passed by, I continued on to the Liberty Cinema. Across the street was a sign that said Management Services, and on it was the same address as that on Bandula's business card. Hesitantly, I went up to the gate.

In front of me was a newly built brick house, painted pink and surrounded by a wall with a black iron gate that opened to a small yard covered with sand. Nervously, I stepped onto the porch and rang the bell, wiping my feet on a thick mat to remove the sand from my shoes. A minute or so went by with no response, and as I was reaching for the bell again a middle-aged woman in a sari appeared at the door.

"I'm looking for Mr. Athukorala," I said respectfully.

"Go upstairs, child. His office is on the second floor," the woman said, pointing to the stairway. I thanked her and followed the stairway up. It was another house converted into an office. The second floor was divided into cubicles and the space next to the top of the stairway was the reception area.

The receptionist was on the phone; her hair fell over her face, her lips shone bright red and her fingers, covered with rings, were playing with a gold chain hanging around her neck.

"Can I help you, miss?"

"I'm here to see Mr. Athukorala," I said.

"Do you have an appointment?"

"No, but he would want to see me," I said uncertainly, hoping it was true, though I couldn't even be sure if he would remember me.

The receptionist looked at me curiously, asked for my name, then pushed the intercom button and told Bandula that Trish was here.

The office was huge, like a conference room, and two men sitting at a long rectangular table pointed to another door, which I walked through, feeling a little awkward in the formal surroundings.

He was looking down at the street, talking on the phone, and I stood just inside the door waiting for him to turn around. It was a spacious, plush room—a glass wall with long lace curtains, a cream-colored couch with a side table and a gleaming red-cement floor. I'll have to be careful walking on that polished floor in my high heels, I thought. His desk, made of teak, had a mirror finish and kidney-shaped top; alongside it was a bookshelf with a vase of bright red Anthuriums.

When he hung up and turned around, his eyes widened and his mouth dropped open. "Ranga! Is that really you?" he said. A wave of relief passed through me, and I walked toward him with a smile.

"Yes."

"Indra told me your name was Trish. Have you changed your name?"

Though he looked and talked like the Bandula I had met on the way to Lebanon nineteen months before, in these plush surroundings he seemed so superior to me that I wasn't comfortable calling him by his first name.

"No, sir, it's my middle name, sorry about the confusion. I wanted to surprise you."

"You surprised me, all right. Please take a seat." He pointed to one of the cushioned armchairs in front of his desk and sank into his executive swivel chair. Still surprised, he spoke into the intercom and told Indra to hold all his calls and send us some tea. He studied me for a few seconds, then leaned back in his chair and said, "I read about you in the papers. I tried to find you. Where were you, when did you get back, and what really happened?"

I smiled, trying to decide which question to answer first. "I've been back for about a year," I finally said. "My parents moved to Negombo to give me a fresh start."

That was all I could say; the words stopped in my throat.

"You don't have to talk about it right now. I understand what you must have gone through," he said. His voice was so gentle and kind, I felt as if I was insulting him.

"I'm sorry, sir," I blurted out. "It's not that I don't trust you, I just want to leave my past behind me and start my life over."

He leaned forward, resting his arms on the desktop.

"I'm so glad you came to see me, that means so much."

"So, tell me," he went on, "what can I do to help you now?"

He sounded so sincere that it was easy to present my request. "I know I didn't listen to you in the plane back then. If I had, things would have been very, very different. Well, I'm here now, and if your offer of work still stands I'd like to take it."

He walked over to the side table just as an office attendant came in with a tray of tea, biscuits and crackers. The attendant placed the tray on the table and was going to pour when Bandula stopped him and asked him to leave.

Bandula made two cups of tea with sugar and cream, handed me one and asked me to join him on the couch. I sat on the edge of the couch, sipping my tea, wondering if he had heard me.

Finally, he said, "I have a friend who's in need of a secretary. I can train you if you're willing to try."

"I will, sir, and I'll do my best," I said quickly, before he could change his mind.

"I know you will," he said.

I couldn't understand why he was so nice to me. What was in it for him?

"I'd like you to start next Monday," he went on. "I'll pay you five hundred rupees a month."

Too excited to speak, I just sat there, shedding tears of happiness. Bandula watched me patiently.

It took me a while to pull myself together. When I did, I thanked him for giving me a chance to start my life over.

At last, I had found my way to independence. Five hundred rupees didn't take me to the castle of my dreams, but it was a good start. Every morning I was wakened by Amma softly whispering in the dark, "Wake up, it's five o'clock," and gently shaking me. I would place a pillow next to my son—Samadha, five years old now, still shared the room with me—and quietly slip out of bed.

After a cold shower I would sip hot tea and get dressed in one of Amma's out-of-fashion saris, then tuck my hair up in a knot and apply a little lipstick and some jasmine perfume to both sides of my neck. With another cup of tea and one or two string hoppers, a type of pasta, in my stomach, I would take one last peak at my dreaming child and set off to work.

The narrow roads of Negombo had no sidewalks and were strewn with rotten food, fruit and animal waste. Pedestrians, beggars and stray animals owned the road, and trying to dodge oncoming vehicles I never knew if I would knock into someone or fall into one of the smelly open gutters that ran alongside the road. I had to take my time, because if I walked too fast my knees would buckle.

Once at the bus stand, I would join the long line of people waiting to get to the city. I had to allow extra time to wait for a less crowded bus, because if I couldn't sit down on the ride in, my back would hurt for the rest of the day.

I grew familiar with the crowd that traveled with me each day and smiled at them, acknowledging their presence, but not wanting anyone to probe into my past, I avoided making friends. Men often seized the opportunity to rub up against women on the crowded bus. I carried a safety pin and pricked any man who tried that with me.
Nelum, Bandula's secretary, taught me all the skills I would need to be a personal secretary and became a good friend. Some days I worked at the reception desk, other

days as a typist. Bandula and I developed a strictly professional relationship. After that day I first sought him out at the office, we never had any personal conversation again, and we distanced ourselves from each other. It made me sad to lose him as a friend, but I had to accept this situation to prevent needless gossip.

Bandula's wife, Mrs. Athukorala, was the company accountant. She was a nice person but she didn't trust me with Bandula. If he walked in to the reception area, she would stare at me to make sure I wasn't looking at her husband. She made me so uncomfortable that I actually felt as if I was having an affair with him.

As for my coworkers, they had read the newspaper account—Bandula had shared it with them when the story first came out—and though no one questioned me about anything, they too focused their watchful eyes on me. Some male workers passed me dirty notes and one invited me to move in with him. The women whispered with each other if they saw me talking with a man.

I chose my words carefully and pretty much stuck to myself, remaining in the office at lunch break and at the end of the day going straight to the bus. Nelum was my only friend.

My parents gave me security, my job gave me skills, and my son gave me the will to be strong. Part of my pay went to my parents, to cover lodging, while the rest provided for Samadha's and my needs. Samadha was enrolled in the same coed school that I had attended as a child. Meanwhile Pappa, living close to Colombo now, was getting more patients and making more money. The Money that Lebanese driver had given me at the airport paid off my mother's loan and I was free of debt.

And, of course, I was still married. Now that I had the money and the courage to go to court, I hired a lawyer and quietly and legally ended my marriage to Tilak.

Nelum offered to teach me shorthand and invited me to her home. A Burgher woman whose husband worked in Dubai, she lived with her parents, her younger brother and her married older sister. I started visiting every weekend. Some days Samadha came along and we would spend the night at Nelum's house.

Nelum had shared my Lebanon story with her family and I had no control over how they judged me. I didn't like the looks her younger brother and his friends gave me, and I pretended to ignore them.

One afternoon I was heading home from Nelum's when Ajith, a friend of her brother's, showed up at the bus stop. It didn't surprise me—sooner or later one of them was bound to make a move—and I was ready for him.

"Do you have to go home tonight?" he asked, leering.

"What do you mean?" I asked, hiding my anger.

"Let's go some place. I'd like to spend some time with you."

I wanted to slap his face, but I didn't want to lose the only friend I had. "I'm a mother, Ajith, not a slut. I don't sleep around. Men are the last thing on my mind."

"Don't try to act so innocent. I know your character, you can't pretend with me."

"You might think you know all about me, but you're wrong," I said, trying my best to be calm and not make a scene. "Even if all that you heard about me is true, why would I want to waist my time with a punk like you?"

"Oh, now I'm not good enough for the princess?" he said. His annoyed tone scared me. As a Sri Lankan woman I had no power over a man; I had to end it quickly and safely to avoid trouble.

"I'm sorry to disappoint you, Ajith," I said in the nicest voice I could muster. "I'm not the woman you think I am, please go home, I won't tell any of this to Nelum if you leave now. I want to continue my friendship with her—please don't ruin that."

"Well, *nangi*, since you asked me nicely I'll leave, but don't be so sure of yourself."

I was a woman without a man, and a bad reputation that seemed impossible to shed. All I could do was hide my past and try to build a new future. I tried to act like a role model, avoiding all contact with men—not even looking at them. I listened more and spoke less, smiled when I wanted to laugh, and held my tongue when in doubt. It wasn't easy but I worked hard at it.

Despite these efforts, Amma kept a close eye on me. Once I left the office a bit late and missed my bus. Like a teenager, I was afraid of being late, worried that my mother wouldn't trust me. When the bus arrived in Negombo it was dark and as I was walking home I recognized a shadow a couple of yards ahead walking toward me.

"What took you so long?" Amma said. When I explained what had happened, she said, "What is so important that you have to work late? Did anyone else stay in the office with you?"

Not wanting to hurt Amma's feelings or do anything to upset her, I patiently answered all her questions. But I was angry about her suspicions and hated being treated like a child. My life was circumscribed by the house and the walls that surrounded it; I needed friends other than my parents to fill the gaps in my life. I thought about Berny, the only male friend from my youth. He was the kind of person I needed to talk to, someone who would listen and not judge. When I tried to locate him, however, I found out that he had left the country.

Excruciating back pain limited my activities, but I learned to live with it and go beyond my limitations without showing signs of discomfort or disability. Though I wasn't physically normal, I wanted to look it.

Hotel Thunderbird was a three-story building on a heavily trafficked stretch of Galle Road, near a liquor store and an ice cream vendor. It had no parking lot, not even a bellboy to open the door for guests, and I doubted if I had the right address. It was nothing like the grand hotels in Colombo—the Galle Face, Hilton, Tajmahal and Oberoi—but I consoled myself with the thought that someday I would have a chance to work in one of them. This was only the beginning.

Head held high, shoulders back, I strode inside. At the front desk a male receptionist greeted me, asked me to take a seat and reached for the phone.

I sat down on a couch and waited anxiously for my first job interview. Behind the reception desk were pigeonholes that held the keys and the mail to each room. Two palm plants stood in off in the corner, and a stairway led to the upper floors.

Bandula had offered to train me to work for his friend. The training period was supposed to have lasted just a month, but three months had gone by and he hadn't mentioned his friend again. Perhaps the man had found another secretary, I thought. And so, unhappy being around suspicious coworkers at Management Services, with Nelum's help I had begun looking for new jobs. I hadn't told Bandula I was planning to leave his office and I felt guilty about it. Still, my spirits lifted when my applications brought two responses. One of them was a receptionist position at the Thunderbird Hotel.

A young man came down the stairs and without any introduction asked me to follow him to the main office on the second floor. In his office, he handed me some typing paper and two handwritten letters and showed me to a typewriter. "Type those letters," he said, and sat at his desk. The letters were easy to read, and I typed them quickly as he checked my speed. He then introduced me to the personnel manager, Mr. Abeysekera.

Mr. Abeysekera, a middle-aged man with a big stomach, reminded me so much of my father that I felt at ease in front of him. Smiling politely, he showed me to a chair in front of his huge table. He raised his chin and adjusted his red-striped tie, then looked at my resume and the typing results.

"I see that you are from Negombo. Are you close to town?" he asked.

"On the main street near Maristella College."

"Oh," he sighed, "I'm from Negombo too. Traveling back and forth from that far away isn't going to be easy. Do you think you can manage it?"

"No problem, sir. My present job is in Colpetty, and I've been commuting for a few months now."

He questioned me about my job, why I was leaving, the flexibility of my time and so forth. The interview went on for about twenty minutes.

"I think you would be the perfect candidate for this position," he said, and paused. "I'd like to offer you the job."

Speechlessly, with trembling hands, I stared back at him, then dropped my eyes, trying to hide my excitement.

"I can pay you seven hundred and fifty rupees a month. The service charge would average another two or three hundred rupees during the season."

"What is a service charge?"

"The guests pay a service charge on their bills, and we distribute that among all employees each month. You also get meals during work hours."

Stunned, I felt as if I had won a sweepstakes. I accepted his offer and he gave me a tour of the hotel. One half of the first floor was rented out to other businesses; the other half was set up for the reception area and kitchen. The offices, the housekeeping department, the restaurant and a hair salon were on the second floor. Half of the second floor and the entire third floor were guestrooms.

After being introduced to the head receptionist, I left the hotel bubbling with joy. My second interview was at a small import-export company. Although I had accepted the offer at the hotel, I was curious to know what this other job would pay.

It was a small, professional-looking company. I sat again for a typing and math test, and the manager was pleased with my results. He explained the job to me. "Starting pay would be eight hundred rupees, but you would get a raise in three months." He paused. "This is a good company to work for. I have a few more interviews today, but I'd like you to call me tomorrow." He gave me his card and after thanking him I left.

In both appointments I had done well. I liked the looks of the import-export company and the manager's professional manner. It was also right in Colombo—only one bus ride away. Still, the hotel job excited me.

Thrilled with my success, I felt the need to share my joy with someone. It was only two in the afternoon and at the bus stop there wasn't anyone who looked familiar. I saw a young man with his face buried in a paper who resembled Berny. He leaned forward to see if any buses were coming, then looked around and saw my eyes on him. We stared at each other for a second, then he went back to his paper.

The bus was almost empty, but without giving it a second thought I boldly sat down beside the young man, throwing all my former caution to the wind. He glanced at me out of the corner of his eyes and continued to read. It was hot; my clothes were sticking to me. As the bus accelerated I turned to him and asked if he wouldn't mind opening the window.

"Oh, sure," he said, opened the window, then turned back to me and asked, "Do you want the corner seat?"

His words didn't register; I was too excited. Instead I blurted out, "I got a job!"

Raising his eyebrows, he looked at me with amusement. "Oh, yes? Do you want the corner seat?" he asked again.

Now I heard him. Of course there were plenty of empty seats, and yet he was offering me his corner seat.

"Do you mind?" I asked innocently.

He replied with a smile, and after we switched places he folded his paper, laid it on his lap and turned to me. "So, tell me about your job," and gladly I shared my triumph with him. He asked me where I lived, and told me that he was from a small town, a few miles north of Negombo. I found myself chattering away to him as if I had known him all my life.

His name was Nuwan. He worked as a computer operator as a private contractor to a company in Colombo. "They give me a week off every six months when they renew my contract," he said. He lived with his mother and father—both teachers—grandmother and a younger brother and sister, who were still in school. We continued our conversation all the way to Negombo. Before parting we exchanged work numbers and he said he wouldn't be back to work for a week. I left him at the Negombo bus stand, where he would take the next bus home..

Walking home, I had a nagging feeling that I had done something wrong. Was I really a bad person? I regretted talking to him and giving him my work number. I had said too much, I thought, and wished that he would never cross my path again. A friendship with a male would only bring more shame, and I had to protect myself from that. My only consolation was that after a month I would be at a different work number, and he wouldn't be able to contact me.

When I reached home, Samadha was perched on top of the concrete pole that held the gate. I hugged him and said, "Ammy got a new job, Putha, now I can buy you more toys and send you to a better school."

"I want to go to Marist Stella," he said. It was the best private boy's school in Negombo, maintained by the Marist brothers. Every rich boy in the neighborhood went to that school, but not being a Catholic, my son had no chance of being admitted there. "We'll see," I said, not wanting to disappoint him, and carried him into the living room.

My mother was laughing at something Pappa had said. My father, one leg over the arm of the chair, was tightening his sarong over his big shaking belly.

They both looked at me. "You're home early, are you okay?" Pappa said.

"She went for some interviews today," Amma said. "How did they go?"

"I got the job at the hotel, and I think I have the other job too," I beamed, and filled them in.

"Why do you look so surprised that you got the job? You can achieve anything if you have the will to try for it," Pappa said.

Going over to him, I laid my head on his stomach and he put his arm around me. He was happy for me.

"You don't know how smart you are," Amma said. "Imagine what you could have accomplished if you had continued your education."

Can't you be happy for what I did accomplish, instead of what I didn't? I thought, but held my tongue and retreated into my room.

"Working in a hotel isn't a respectable job for a woman—you should take the other job," Amma called from the living room.

"Leave her alone," Pappa said.

Amma was right. People looked down on women who worked in hotels. Still, in my heart I wanted that hotel job, and I decided to listen to my heart. Though I was still not a member, I went to church to give thanks to God and praised Him with a solo.

I started to wonder if there was a way to leave my parents and live on my own. Now that I was making a living it seemed almost possible; the idea excited me, and at the same time scared me. What would I do with Samadha when I went to work? And what would I tell my parents? They would fight to keep me forever. But the real question was, would I ever find the courage to break away from them?

At the Pettah bus station everyone ran in all directions, like ants in a colony. I joined a line of impatient people, their faces drawn, their clothes sticking to their bodies. As always, it was going to be a long wait. Fanning myself with a handkerchief, I leaned against a railing to support my aching back. Suddenly I sensed that someone was watching me. Glancing over my shoulder, I spied him through the crowd a few yards away. He wasn't standing in the line. Before I could think, my face broke into a smile.

"I thought it was you," Nuwan said, coming closer. "Didn't you say you weren't working this week?"

"I came to collect my salary, then thought maybe I would see you again," he said.

Was he telling the truth, or had he come just to see me? My hope never to run into him again was in vain; here he was, even before the end of his week off.

"Let's take the private bus," he said. Unlike city buses, private buses didn't have a fixed schedule and, since they cost more money, I hardly ever took them.

Deliberating, I got lost in his long thick eyelashes and handsome eyebrows. He looked straight at me, searching, as if he was trying to read my mind. I had never seen such a pure, innocent look in a man. There was something about him that I couldn't resist, and without weighing the consequences of my actions, I followed him to the private bus stand.

Awkwardly I sat down next to him and tried to carry on a conversation. He was tall and slender, his face long with shallow cheeks and broad cheekbones, and when his thin lips parted in a smile all his tiny squirrel teeth showed. Spellbound, I forgot the Sri Lankan taboo about not befriending males outside of one's family, and enjoyed being seated next to such a handsome man.

He got off the bus with me at Negombo and asked if we could meet that weekend. Ignoring the warning signals in my head, I agreed.

As soon as we parted the same nagging fear and tension returned. My consolation was his look of innocence, and the interest he showed in me. Every time I thought about him it felt as if I was under a spell, and hard as I fought against my emotions, my will was weak. A sense of wild abandon seized me; I wanted to live in the moment, to revel in the excitement of romance—for I knew it would end even before it started.

The rest of the week was spent restlessly counting the hours until our tryst. I was irritable and scared. Going out on a weekend required a good excuse, and I told Amma I was going to see Nelum. Samadha begged me to come along, and I had a hard time explaining why I couldn't take him with me that day. I didn't feel good lying to my mother and disappointing my son, and my heart questioned my judgment, yet my feelings overpowered my conscience.

Nuwan was waiting for me at the bus stop. Without knowing what we were doing, we got on a bus and headed to Colombo. "What should we do?" I asked him.

"We can go to a movie or to a park, whatever you like," he said, like a teenager. I was embarrassed—it reminded me of my youth, roaming around the park with Berny—and hoping to avoid prying eyes, I asked him if we could take the train round trip to Kalutara, a couple of hours' from the city. He agreed to it.

At the Colombo train station, the loudspeaker announced the train schedule and the platform numbers. "Let's get some tea while we wait," said Nuwan, and I followed him to the canteen like a child, scared and tense. He bought us tea and we sat at a table swatting flies away.

Half an hour later the train arrived at our platform. It being the weekend, there weren't many passengers, and we got an empty compartment and sat next to each other. The back of his short-sleeved brown shirt was damp with sweat. With a handkerchief I mopped the perspiration from my face.

The train made a slow creaking noise as it made its way through towns and villages, stopping at each station. The wooden seats were hard and my back started to hurt. Nuwan was still looking out the window; his hand with its long slender fingers rested on the seat. He crossed his legs and I saw his toes pressed together in his brown sandals; they were long and shapely, like his fingers. He didn't talk much; his mind seemed far away. I wondered how old he could be—was he younger than me?

Suddenly I had an urge to get off the train and run away from him. It felt as if I had been asleep all this time and now I was awake, the spell broken. What am I doing here with this man? I asked myself. "I want to go back," I said thoughtlessly. "I'm not comfortable with this."

"Let's get off at the next station," he said calmly. I thought he would try to convince me to stay but he didn't ask any questions, which impressed me.

We got off at the next stop, almost halfway to Kalutara, and he suggested that we get something to eat at a café. Not wanting to disappoint him again, I agreed, but we both felt ill at ease. I was furious with myself for acting like a teenager. Feeling responsible for the situation, I decided to set things right between us before it got any worse, and I had the perfect exit strategy. It was only fair to let him know the truth about myself. That would scare him away.

I waited until we were heading home. We took the bus rather than the train back. Gathering all my courage, I said, "I need to tell you something—I'm sorry for not saying it earlier."

"What is it?" he asked with his innocent smile.

"I'm a married woman." I paused and looked into his eyes. He didn't freeze, and his eyes didn't widen. Any other man would have given me a piece of his mind and stormed off the bus, but not Nuwan. I had to give it to him straight, make it harder so he would run without looking back.

"I don't live with him anymore, but I have a five-year-old son." Again, he didn't appear to be surprised or threatened, and didn't say a word. What was going on in his head? I wondered, and then began spilling everything. "I look and act like a normal woman but I'm not, there are limits to what I can do. I could never be a normal housewife to any man."

I explained about my spinal surgery and the condition of my back. Calmly, without raising an eyebrow or turning away, he listened.

"What happened—how did you get hurt so badly?" he asked after a long silence.

"I don't want to talk about it. I'm sorry."

"It's okay, I understand. But where is your husband? What happened with him?" I gave him a short version of what had happened to my marriage.

After listening to all that, he kept quiet for a moment, then turned to me and said, "Thank you."

"For what, misleading you?" I said, unable to bear his kindness after what I had done.

"You trusted me with the truth, and I want to do something in return," he said. "I want to introduce you to a good friend of mine."

"I don't want to meet any of your friends. Please don't tell anyone about me."

"He's not just a friend, he's a Jesuit priest. You'll like him. Please come and meet him, just once," he pleaded.

I had great respect for priests. They were the ones who forgave sins. It would be good to get to know a priest, I thought.

"All right," I said, "but you can't tell him what I've told you."

"I promise, but you can tell him anything, you can trust him with your life. He can help you."

"Why do you think I need help?" I said, annoyed.

"Don't be upset. I'm not trying to hurt you in any way."

Who is this man? I wondered again. Why didn't he despise me like the rest of the world?

Suddenly he stood up and rang the bell; I followed him to the exit and we got off in Bambalapitiya, the town next to Colpetty. After a couple of yards on Galle Road we turned into a side street and there ahead of us was the beach. The rough waves shattered when they hit the shore and the salty air fanned our skin, covering us with a film of sticky moisture.

At the end of the street stood the Jesuit House, a two-story building that looked like a boarding house surrounded by a six-foot concrete wall. I followed Nuwan through a side door into the waiting area. Nuwan pointed me to a chair and disappeared down a corridor. Checking my watch, I grew impatient. I wanted to get home as quickly as possible; the whole day had been a waste of time and I regretted the fact that I had lied to Amma.

I heard footsteps and laughter in the corridor and saw Nuwan and a man coming toward me. The man had a cup of tea in his hand. He looked to be in his early forties, wore a baggy shirt, worn khaki trousers and ugly rubber slippers. He must be the priests' helper, I thought. He handed me the cup of tea and sat down in a chair in front of me. They were both still laughing, I couldn't tell why.

"This is Father Devin," said Nuwan. Almost spilling tea on my clothes, I tried to get up. I had expected a tidy person dressed in a white robe with black rope around his waist and proper shoes on his feet. He would have approached me with his head held high, hands in a pious lock, and I would have jumped off my chair and greeted him by saying, "God bless you, Father." Instead, I stared at this ragged man in front of me, dressed like a beggar and too friendly. I wondered if I should say God bless you, but the words didn't come out of my mouth. His eyes were on me, studying me. I wanted to hide from those eyes, but he smiled and I smiled back.

"I'm sorry, I thought you were someone else," I stammered.

They both laughed again. Then Father Devin asked me where I was from and I told him about Pappa once being in a Jesuit seminary. We stayed there for a while, but I had nothing much to say and presently the meeting ended. Before parting Father Devin and I exchanged telephone numbers. Since he was a priest I had nothing to fear in giving him my home phone number; my parents wouldn't mind my having a priest for a friend. Even so, I didn't think he would call or that I would even see him again. I was excited nonetheless to tell Pappa that I had met a Jesuit priest.

On our way back home, Nuwan explained to me that Father Devin was a close family friend whom he'd known since childhood. Now it all made sense—Nuwan, it turned out, was planning to become a Jesuit priest himself, and Father Devin was his role model. That explained his neutral behavior toward my truth, and his desire to help me. It also put me at ease to realize that he wasn't looking for a romantic relationship, that we could just be friends. I thanked God for clearing up the situation, but I was embarrassed for assuming that Nuwan was after me romantically.

So, I thought, I have found another Berny, a real friend who wouldn't judge me by my past. That was comforting, but the world around me hadn't changed. I wouldn't stand a chance of convincing anyone that I could have a male friend without going to bed with him. Unwilling to face another scandal, I decided to continue enjoying Nuwan's friendship—but to be extra careful.

For two more weeks I worked at B.A. Services, and decided to stay home for the rest of the month before starting my new job. As it turned out, Bandula didn't mind my leaving the company. He wished me good luck and asked me to keep in touch, and I thanked him for giving me the foundation for a new life.

Chapter 13

For centuries the Buddhist Sinhalese tradition had a beneficent effect on Sri Lanka, inspiring its stew of ethnic and religious groups to live together in peace. After the island won independence from the British in 1948, however, ethnic rivalries began to heat up.

Of all the troubles that beset the new democracy, the most persistent was call of the minority Tamils for a separate nation. Centuries ago, the Hindu Tamil migrated to Sri Lanka from south India. While Sri Lanka's majority Sinhalese speak a blend of Pali and Sanskrit, the Tamil speak a Dravidian language. This language barrier and the religious divide nurtured in the minority Tamil a sense of separate identity, and the result was civil war throughout the 1980s.

Tension had been simmering for years. Then in 1983 the Liberation Tamil Tigers of Ealem (LTTE), who claimed one third of Sri Lanka as their own, bombed a jeep in Jafna, killing thirteen Sinhalese soldiers. The bodies of the soldiers were brought south to Colombo for burial. After the funerals Sinhalese extremists and other thugs gathered in vigilante groups and ran amok, attacking Tamils and anyone associated with the LTTE, burning down shops, houses and buses and killing many innocent bystanders. Though it lasted only one day, the trouble marked the beginning of the ongoing war.

That day I was working at Hotel Thunderbird. When news of the riots broke we closed the establishment, and all the employees assembled in the restaurant on the second floor to watch the violence unfold in the street. Hoodlums broke into the liquor store next door, got drunk and started attacking Tamils. We had a few Tamil employees at the hotel and we hid them inside the laundry room, then watched in horror as the rioters began hurling themselves against the gate that was the only thing protecting us.

Colombo was in turmoil—fires raging, phone lines dead, roads closed—and it didn't seem as if the government, the police or the army were taking any action to stem the violence. I knew my parents would be worried about my safety, but with no way to send them a message, for hours I stood by the hotel window watching the chaos into which my once peaceful land had descended. While languishing in the hospital in Beirut I had only heard the sound of bombs; now I was seeing with my very own eyes the terrifying effect of violence in action. Fortunately, the gate in front of the Thunderbird held, and the men trying to force their way in eventually gave up, but not before setting fire to two stores on the ground floor that were run by Tamils. They threw kerosene on the merchandise, ignited it, then moved on to other targets. After they disappeared, the hotel security men, aided by several employees, put the fire out, but there was nothing left inside the stores aside from blackened brick walls.

A few hours later, when I was all but resigned to the fact that I might have to spend the night in the hotel, without any assurance that the thugs wouldn't return, murder our poor Tamil coworkers, and exact revenge on us for hiding them, I was surprised to see Nuwan in front of the gate trying to get in.

"Who is he?" my coworkers asked.

"My brother," I blurted out without a second thought, and dashed downstairs to the reception area. The security guard at the gate let him in.

"It would be safer to go home until this violence is over," he said breathlessly.

"How did you get here?"

"Hurry, let's go," he said without answering me, and I ran after him toward a private van that was carrying people.

Though we had been traveling together to work and had become fast friends, Nuwan was the last person I expected to come to my rescue. To collect me he had run all the way from Pettah to Wellawatha, about five miles, then hailed the van. I didn't have the peace of mind to examine his motive; I was just deeply grateful.

We squeezed into the van and the driver took us as far as he could, dropping us off a couple of miles away from the Pettah train station. The whole city was engulfed in smoke. Shops were burning on both sides of the road, people were screaming for help, crying, running for cover as roughnecks with knives and rods roamed the streets, checking every vehicle for Tamils. Looters were jumping through smashed windows, their arms laden with stolen goods.

My back was hurting and I couldn't run, but Nuwan dragged me along. We jumped over dead bodies trying to find transportation home. We could smell burning flesh, saw the faces of men and women on the road who had been burned alive. I didn't look back for fear of being killed should I demonstrate my concern. I was ashamed of my fellow Sinhalese that day and hated the government for not taking action against the violence.

Nuwan pulled me into an overcrowded train where people were hanging out of the windows and huddled on the roof. When we reached Negombo he escorted me home, then hurried back to help his Tamil friends.

I had already introduced Father Devin to my parents, telling them we had met at work one day when he dropped by to visit Bandula. It was a lie, another strand in the web of fabrication I had been spinning at home and at work, but it was a white lie, I reasoned, told to maintain harmony, and therefore acceptable. The truth is, I didn't like lying, and I longed for the day when I could lead my life free of such deception.

At any rate, on that infamous day in Sri Lankan history I had no choice but to introduce Nuwan to my family. My parents were thankful to him for bringing me home safely, but I sensed Amma's suspicion. Why would this young man take such a risk to come to my aid?

"He is a friend of Father Devin's and he wants to be a priest," I insisted. "So he is already acting like one."

That terrifying day made me realize how much Nuwan cared for me; I could count on him for anything. He enjoyed giving and didn't look for anything in return. I had shared with him the story of what happened in Lebanon, including the part about my jump from the balcony, and he accepted me without judgment. Impressed by this and his charity toward others in need, I was drawn to Nuwan and felt completely at ease in his presence.

In return, he shared his own experience with me. "My family suffered in poverty for many generations, and my parents worked hard for the life they enjoy today. They want me to have a taste of what they went through, so that I'll work hard some day too."

"What do you mean?"

"My father has his own house, his own land, and his own business. He is also school teacher. My mother teaches in the same school, so they have enough money. But they don't want things to come easily for me," he continued. "One day in school, during recess, I hid my pencil under a tree while playing with my friends. Later, when I couldn't find it, my father caned me in front of all the students."

"For losing a pencil?"

"Yes. I never ask my parents for anything. My grandmother is the one who buys things for me. She's the one who notices when there are holes in my shirts or my pants."

"Do they treat your brother and sister the same way?"

"No, just me. I'm supposed to set an example to my younger siblings and the whole neighborhood."

Though Nuwan was a gentle, generous person, he wasn't at all close to his parents. They treat him with excessive harshness, I thought, glad to be the one to console him.

With Nuwan's encouragement, I started dropping in on Father Devin. They both believed in helping others without any expectation of reward, and in a bad situation they always looked on the positive side.

Whenever I visited Father Devin he always made me feel special. He never turned me away or kept me waiting, and I found myself talking easily to him, sharing my past, my worries, my fears, as we sat in the visitors' room for hours. Years of shame had made me believe that I wasn't a good person, and guilt kept me hidden from my true self. Rather than judging, he advised me.

When I doubted myself, he would say, "Don't be so hard on yourself, *kelle,* " which meant girl. "You're a good mother." Father Devin taught me to trust myself again, to recognize the real person inside.

"No one is perfect, everyone makes mistakes—that' how you learn. You have to forgive yourself. Remember, you're human."

I was a lost soul trying to hide from my past while still buried in it, and he encouraged me to be independent and take control of my life. I respected him as a priest and loved him as a person.

One day I invited Father Devin and Nuwan home. My parents enjoyed their company. They liked Nuwan, and Pappa and Father Devin got along well; Pappa told him about the old days when he was at the Jesuit seminary. Nuwan and Samadha also took to one another. From that day on, Nuwan and Father Devin became our family friends.

One payday I went to visit Father Devin. Handing me a cup of tea, he asked me if I had a bank account.

I laughed. "Why would I need a bank account? I keep all my money at home, hidden between my clothes." Only businessmen needed bank accounts and checkbooks, I thought. After all, I was paid in cash, and shops didn't accept checks anyway.

Surprised at my answer, he got out of his chair. "Let's go to a bank right now. I'm going to open an account for you."

Not daring to question him—one superior to me—I followed Father Devin to the bank. He filled out some papers, asked me to sign in several places, and at the counter I was given a book that had both his name and mine.

"Every month I need fifty rupees from your pay," he said. "I don't care what expenses you have, you will give me fifty rupees, and I will deposit it into your account."

Why is this so important? I wondered, and as if reading my mind, he said,

"I'm teaching you how to save for your future. I'll keep track of what's happening until you get used to this. Trust me, you'll never regret it."

From that day on I gave Father Devin fifty rupees every month, and as time went on and my bank balance grew I stopped needing encouragement. I learned to follow a budget and save.

Father Devin told me a lot about Nuwan. His age, for one. Just as I had thought, he was younger than I—a whole six years—and that made me uncomfortable. I was battling my feelings for Nuwan, and trying to keep him from falling in love with me. I told Father Devin how we met each day, and confessed my fear of his falling in love with me.

"Don't you worry about that," he said. "He's a good person, his heart is in the right place, and he only wants to help you. Why not enjoy his friendship?"

"He's such a wonderful friend, Father, but I don't want to give him false hope and hurt him."

"I know him well and he trusts me; whenever he meets with you, he comes straight to me and shares all his feelings. He tells me everything."

Everything! That's odd, I thought, remembering the last time we had met. I was sick and burning with fever when I met Nuwan going back home after work one evening. We always occupied the back corner seat to avoid attention. Suddenly I got the chills, and hiding my hand in his, I rested my heavy head on his shoulder and slept all the way to Negombo. When we got off the bus he offered to walk me home, but I wanted to avoid being seen with him in my neighborhood, so I declined.

He walked me to the junction where my street began. As I said goodbye our eyes met and it was as if every cell in my body was waking up. His eyes were pure, nakedly inviting, and I saw his untouched heart opening up to me, showing me how much he loved me. We were so close to each other that I felt his warm breath on me, my lips trembled and ached to feel his touch, but I shoved my feelings aside and moved away. When I turned back he was watching me and I waved at him and kept waving until I reached home. Shame on me, I thought, how could I feel this way toward him?

Had Nuwan shared that moment with Father Devin? It was a shocking awakening for me; no matter what I wanted to believe and what I tried to deny, I realized that Nuwan loved me, we had a connection, and it was not just friendship. It was only a matter of time before I gave in to my own feelings. I had to fight it with everything I had. The age difference, his dream of being a priest, my own desire to be an independent single mother—these were just a few things to consider. And so marriage never crossed my mind. Samadha was the center of my world and I wanted to live for him alone, to provide him with a good life. Moreover, I had a bad back—I would never make a good wife.

I needed the strength to keep some distance between Nuwan and myself. I was tempted to share my thoughts with Father Devin, to seek his advice on how to avoid the unavoidable, but what would he think of me? Falling for a younger man, what kind of woman would do that?

I'll fight it alone, I won't give in, I thought.

During all these transformations in my life, I didn't forget my son. I gave Samadha everything he needed and tried to be a good mother. For his seventh birthday I invited all the children from church and school and gave him a grand party.

After the cake was cut, Samadha wandered off and sat by himself in the yard.

"What's wrong, Putha, aren't you happy?" I said. He looked into my eyes with such sadness that it broke my heart.

"Ammy, I feel so lonely," he said. At once I knew what he meant. Two years had gone by since he'd last seen his father. Tilak hadn't taken me up on my request that he make regular visits, and I wasn't inclined to bother him if he didn't feel the need to see his son.

"Do you miss your father?" I asked, my arms around his shoulders. Tears filled his eyes, and without answering he ran inside the house.

That was it. With no idea where Tilak lived, I sent a couple of letters to his mother's house asking him to visit his son, but never heard back.

Samadha needed a father. No matter what I did, pleasing him became impossible. He spent much of his time gazing into space. His teachers complained that he was in another world, that he hardly made any friends and never laughed. I recognized the lost look in his eyes, felt the pain in his little heart, and tried to get him involved in team sports, but nothing worked.

Pappa loved him dearly and treated him like his own child, but it wasn't enough.

After discussing the issue with Father Devin, he tried to get Samadha to open up to him, but the boy didn't trust anyone. Finally Father Devin offered to take Samadha to see his father.

One promising day, the priest came to our doorstep and asked Samadha to join him for a ride, and off they went on Father Devin's new red motorbike. To avoid any disappointment we had decided not to tell Samadha where he was going. I had given Tilak's mother's address to Father Devin, still not sure where my husband was living.

Within a few hours they came back, and Samadha didn't look as happy as I had hoped.

"I found him, all right," said Father Devin. "I left Samadha on the side of the road and went to the door. He's married; they have a child, a little girl, and she was playing out in the yard. I asked him to come with me to the road, where Samadha was waiting for him, but Tilak was angry with me for bringing the boy to his place."

"Didn't he talk to Samadha?"

"Yes, but he made it very quick. I think he was worried his wife would see them. Still, he promised Samadha he would visit him next week at your house."

"Are you sure he's going to come?"

"He promised."

Samadha counted the days until his father showed up, while I worried that he would be disappointed again. Early in the morning of the appointed day he woke up, dressed in clean pants and a shirt and sat on the steps, waiting with a happy, hopeful look.

"Come and eat your breakfast, I made your favorite *rotti*," Amma called.

"I'm not hungry, Chamma," he said with a hint of excitement, his eyes locked on the pathway. I sat next to him for couple of hours. When lunchtime came, Amma called him again.

"Your lunch is getting cold, you need to eat something now."

"I'll eat with my father, he'll be here any second," Samadha said with assurance. As the minutes dragged on, my doubt grew. Pretending as if everything was all right, I went on with my activities, but my eyes yearned for a glimpse of Tilak.

Slowly the hours dragged. Samadha's bottom must have turned numb along with his trusting heart. The sun was setting, the night insects began to sing and still he kept his station at the doorstep, holding onto the slightest hope that his father would emerge through the bushes. He sighed, his warm breath carrying his sorrow, but he didn't shed a single tear.

"Oh, how I wish my love was enough for you," I whispered to myself, vowing that if I couldn't be a father to him, at least I would make a great father out of him.

At the end of the day I took Samadha inside, tucked him in bed and held him close. "Tomorrow I'll take you to see him," I said, kissing his forehead.

"No, Ammy, I don't think I want to see him ever again, if he doesn't want to see me. I don't want to be a problem to his new family. When I grow up to be a great man, one day I'll pay him a visit."

Samadha never mentioned his father to me again.

I tried to send my son to the Adventist boarding school to give him an English education, but the mission rejected his application since I was no longer a member of the church. Once again I turned to Father Devin for help. He suggested that I get Samadha christened as a Catholic and enroll him in the Marist Stella School, the one he had been dreaming about attending. I followed this advice, and the change my boy needed. He took piano lessons, joined the school band, became a Scout and participated in sports. At last Samadha began enjoying life again.

My job at the hotel was working out well. Greeting visitors, renting rooms and smiling at passersby made the day go quickly. I worked in the office sometimes, but my place was at the reception desk. Kumar, the head receptionist, taught me how to check guests in and out and to keep the accounts. I worked the morning shift but occasionally had to cover other shifts, in which case I was given a room to spend the night. My relationship with the hotel staff was good, I enjoyed their company, male and female, and no one gave me dirty looks or cared who my friends were. That was partly because no one knew I was a mother, let alone a single mother. To avoid gossip and earn respect, I pretended to be a virgin.

I took various courses to hone my skills. One of them was a hotel reception course, where I came in first out of a class of thirty. The company that conducted the course offered me a job in a five-star hotel, and so after one year of service at the Hotel Thunderbird I joined the Beach Hotel as a typist. It was a large, lovely hotel on the beach with two hundred rooms, two fine restaurants and a nightclub. The pay and the benefits were generous. I worked in the office as a typist during the week, and on weekend nights as a receptionist, spending the night at the hotel, and within a few months I was promoted to a position as the personnel manager's assistant.

Meanwhile, Nuwan and I were growing closer, despite my resolve to keep distance between us. My parents loved him. Even though between them Pappa and Amma had twelve children, Nuwan became the son they could count on. He made them laugh, helped my mother when she needed a pair of strong arms and listened to my father's never-ending stories.

To fulfill one of my dreams, he introduced me to a singing group and I joined them to sing at church festivals and weddings. It was one more generous gesture for which I was deeply indebted.

No matter what ground rules I had in mind for our relationship, they all disappeared when I was in Nuwan's presence. Though he wanted to be a priest, which meant a life of celibacy, he never denied his feelings for me or tried to hide them from anyone.

"I want to introduce you to my friends," he said.

Here I was trying to hide from everyone, and he wanted to expose me to the world. "Please don't talk about me with anyone," I pleaded. "People will laugh at you."

"Why do you think like that? You're beautiful and a wonderful person, I want to show them how lucky I am to have you in my life."

I couldn't help laughing. "That's where you're wrong, Nuwan. I'm a woman, a mother, not a virgin. No man would be proud to be my friend."

"Who cares what people think? That doesn't bother me. When I look at you all I see is a little girl, and I'm proud to stand beside her and tell the whole world she's my girl. You're a treasure to me, don't you know that?"

Though we weren't romantically involved, Nuwan considered me his girl. He didn't believe it was wrong to love me and be a priest at the same time.

"Real love is to love the person for who they are," he went on. "It doesn't make any difference to me what you did in the past. I love you as a person, and nothing you do or say will ever change that."

His words were like water sprinkled on a dry seed. A tiny hope was forming inside me. Maybe his nurturing love and trust could bring the seed into the light again. For him, with him, everything seemed possible. No strings attached, no demands made, just his love no matter what.

Little did we know the troubles that lay ahead.

Chapter 14

One fine afternoon, Father Devin called me at work and asked me to stop by on my way home. The tone in his voice disturbed me so I took a half day's leave and went to see him.

"Did you hear from Nuwan?" he said, handing me a cup of tea in the visitors' area.

"No, not today. What's wrong, Father?"

"Nuwan's parents came to see me. They've heard about the two of you."

An alarm went off in my head.

"They came to get information about you," he said.

"What did you tell them?"

"Nothing. They know that you're divorced and that you have a son. I told them that nothing was going on between the two of you. They didn't believe me. They were angry with me for not telling them where you live."

"Why do they want to know where I live?"

"They're furious. I don't know what they're planning to do, but it's safer to stay away from Nuwan for a few days."

"Yes, Father, this is what I was afraid would happen. I'll do anything to stay out of trouble."

"Am I right when I said nothing was going on between you two?" he asked.

"Yes, Father, we're just friends," I said.

We did love each other, but only in our hearts—and even that sort of love was risky in Sri Lanka. Nuwan in his innocence hadn't understood what I meant when I asked him not to discuss me with his friends. Inevitably, the news reached his home.

A couple of days later Nuwan came to our house. He looked exhausted and the light in his eyes was gone. He was suffering from a headache, and Pappa wasn't home to treat him, so Amma gave him a home remedy. He moaned with pain, and my mother let him rest in our guestroom.

"One of my friends told my parents that I was having an affair with a divorced woman," he told me. "My father hit me with a bat and demanded that I never see you again, and locked me up in my room for the last couple of days. I had to see you, so I sneaked out after my parents went to work. My grandmother must be looking for me now."

"How can they still hit you? You're not a child anymore."

"You don't know how cruel they really are. They like to hit me, that's their gift to me as parents. The only person who loved and cared for me was my grandmother. She has been both mother and father to me all these years. I still live there because of her. I can't leave her."

He looked pale, and when I put my hand over his forehead it was very hot. I soaked a cotton pad in vinegar and laid it on his forehead.

"I can't forget the way you accepted me," he said. "Samadha is so lucky to have you for a mother. I wish I had a mother like you."

"Any mother would love her children. How could she not?" I asked.

Mockingly, he laughed. "Not my parents. They don't know what love is. I can't remember a single moment sitting on my mother's lap or listening to her kind words. All they do is yell and hit me. They want me to be someone I'm not. Nothing I do is good enough for them.

"Do they approve of you wanting to be a priest?"

"Yes, only because having a priest in the family will bring them respect."

No wonder he had turned to a stranger for love—to me. That explained everything.

"I'm tired of trying to win their love, tired of trying to impress them. I hate them. But they're still my parents, and I love them too," he continued.

Poor Nuwan, I thought. How could his parents be so cruel to him? Why couldn't they see what a wonderful son they had? I ached for him but was disturbed by his parents' behavior. He wasn't in any shape to go back home, so Amma let him spend the night in our house.

The next day when I came home from work, Amma said that Nuwan's parents had dropped by. They had told my parents that I was having an affair with their son, and had asked them to keep me away from him. Nuwan was still in the house and had heard the conversation.

"Did they know Nuwan was here at the time?"

"He sneaked out the back door, I don't think they saw him, but I felt very guilty," Amma said, angry at his parents for coming to our doorstep to accuse me. "I don't want him anywhere near this house again. They were mean, they acted like low-caste, ignorant people who have no respect for anyone." She softened her voice and said,

"Nuwan is a wonderful young man, and I know you don't have many friends, but please don't see him again."

I was angry with them, too, for hurting Nuwan and for dragging my parents into this. Taking Father Devin's advice, I had already decided to stay away from Nuwan, but the trouble had begun.

The next day when I got off the bus from work, Amma was waiting for me. "What's wrong?" I asked, alarmed.

"They're back," she snapped. "They want to talk to you. I'm worried, I came to warn you."

"Why do they want to see me?" I said.

"They're not nice people. Don't make them angry, just agree to anything they say and get rid of them quickly."

What have I gotten into? I asked myself. I went home, trembling from head to toe. The picture Nuwan had given me of his parents was not a pretty one. From the gate I saw them sitting on the front veranda. The father somewhat resembled his son; he was tall and thin, but darker than Nuwan, and his face was clouded over with hatred. Nuwan's mother was short and heavy with a round, harsh face.

My throat was dry and I called out to Amma for a glass of water. I forced a smile, sat down in front of them and leaned back to soothe my aching back. My mother brought the water and as I took it my fingers trembled. Quickly I set the glass down to hide my fear from them.

"We're Nuwan's parents, and we want to talk to you about him," the mother said. "There are some rumors in our town that he is having an affair with a divorced woman. Let me tell you how we heard this." She adjusted her heavy bottom on the cane seat and began waving her fleshy hands in the air. "I was in church, and one of his close friends came to me and said, 'Aunty, I have to tell you this before it's too late: Nuwan is having an affair with a divorced woman. First I thought he was only fooling around but now I think he is very serious about this woman. She is an older woman with a child, and I don't want to see his life destroyed.'"

When I heard this I started shaking, and thought I was going to faint. "How could this happen to my child?" Nuwan's mother moaned. "Then I realized how his behavior has changed. He never comes home on time, and he stopped giving his monthly pay to me. He has no money anymore, he spent it all on you. Please stop this! You are a mother, you should understand how a mother feels when something bad is happening to her child. This is wrong, he is too young! His life has not even started yet, please don't destroy it!"

I hated her for coming to my house and talking to me with such anger, and felt a sudden urge to defend myself. "First of all, I make my own living, and I don't take money from anyone. Nuwan and I are only friends. What's wrong with that?"

"Find another friend and leave my child alone!" she lashed out.

"Who are you to order me around?" I said, throwing caution to the wind. "You should control your son, not me. Ask him to stay away from me."

"Don't you worry," the father said, "if you won't put an end to it, I'll do it for you. Just be careful you don't get caught with him." With that, they stood up and stormed off.

Shaken to the core, I watched them disappear down the road, feeling their invisible hands around my neck. I couldn't face my parents. Why did I always get into trouble, why couldn't I give my poor parents a break?

Nuwan and I meant a lot to each other. His love and care had filled the empty space inside my heart, and my love had done the same for him. But was it worth it—for the sake of platonic love, to get into a battle with his parents and hurt my own in the process? I wasn't going to risk destroying the world I had built for Samadha by adding more disorder to my life. I decided to meet with Nuwan one last time and ask him to stay away from me until the situation calmed down. I also had to warn him about his parents; if they caught us together, the consequences would be terrible for him.

After a sleepless night, I rose early and got ready for work. It was around five in the morning when I set off down the road. The ground was wet from morning dew, the dogs barked and a few yards away I heard the sound of a vehicle. The moon was still shining. Glancing over my shoulder to make sure no one was following me, I walked toward the bus station in the darkness. Nuwan was waiting for me in his usual place behind the Colombo bus line, and anxiously I went over to him.

"We have to hurry, your parents might be watching us!" I whispered, and started running toward the private bus with Nuwan following me. We went all the way to the back and sat at the window seat. Nervously I waited for the engine to start, but before it did Nuwan's father came charging onto the bus and headed straight toward the back where we were sitting. I thought he was going to hit Nuwan; instead, he started yelling like a lunatic.

"So this is what you do every day, guarding this whore as she goes back and forth to work, spending all your hard-earned money trying to please her! Look at this bitch sitting with my son, looking so innocent as if she can't even count to three. I know who you are, you rotten slut, go find another rotten dog to satisfy your filthy body."

Outrageously, he went on with his obscene accusation, insulting me in the crowded bus with everyone listening.

Nuwan didn't say a word. He just sat there like a child with his head down, listening to his father's insults. It all happened quickly, but it seemed as if it went on forever. Finally, Nuwan stood up and got out of the bus with his father close on his heels.

Outside, his father continued his public tirade, pointing at me through the window.

"Look at that tramp! She is a mother with no shame! She must be sixty years old but she's looking for young boys to drink their blood! She is an insult to motherhood! Take a good look at her," he went on, addressing the passengers, "and keep your sons away from her!"

I felt as if I were up on a stage naked, with people throwing stones at me. All I wanted was for the ground to open up and swallow me. Closing my eyes to avoid any eye contact, I waited for the bus to move; it was taking forever. Finally the engine started rumbling, the wheels turning, and the screaming voice of Nuwan's father faded away.

The bus was full and I sensed the tension in the crowd, felt their stares making holes in me, and rising from my seat, I rang the bell and got off at the next bus stop. I stood there, shaking with shame and anger, wondering what to do next. My strength was drained, I couldn't go to work. The only place I would be safe was at the Jesuit House with Father Devin. So I got onto another bus and made my way there.

As I walked in Father Devin was with another visitor, but right away he saw the expression on my face. "What's wrong?" he said as I stared at him, unable to find words. He walked over to me and I looked away, trying to hold back my tears. "Go upstairs, I'll be right with you," he said, and I headed toward the stairs. A few minutes later he joined me.

"What happened, Kelle?" he asked, and I burst out crying.

When I collected myself, I told him what had happened in the bus.

"I can't go back to that town, Father. I can't go home!" I said.

"Don't worry about it right now, we'll figure something out," he said calmly, and offered me tea.

How could I face my parents or my son? I had to stay away from them for at least a day. Father Devin offered to get a room for me at the local convent until I was ready to go home.

"I'll make a trip to your house to get you some clothes and tell your parents that you're all right," he said.

How grateful I was to have a friend like Father Devin, whom my parents trusted!

"Don't worry about what anyone says," he reassured me. "They don't know you, they haven't had a chance to get to know you. You're a good mother, a loving person—believe it in your heart, don't let anyone tell you what you are or what you aren't, or what to do or how to feel. Listen to your own heart. Don't give the world so much power; keep the control switch of your life in your hands."

That was just what I needed to hear. Still, I didn't feel as if I could ever face the people in my hometown of Negombo again. I called in sick and didn't go to work for three days, stayed at the convent and received a daily visit from Father Devin. I was afraid to go near my house or into town alone, thinking Nuwan's parents would hurt me. I regretted getting involved with Nuwan and was angry with him for not coming to my defense on the bus; at the same time I felt sorry for him, having suffered a lifetime with such parents. In the meantime, Father Devin had asked Nuwan to stay away from me.

When I did go back to work, the security guard at the gate stopped me. “Madam, there was a man here looking for you. He said you were married and that you have a son. He also said that you were having an affair with his son who is younger than you. He wanted to see the manager, but I sent him away asking him to make an appointment. He asked me if anyone visited you here, and I told him it was only your cousin. Do you know him, madam?”

“I don’t know who you’re talking about, he must be a nut case,” I said, hiding my fear. Ignoring his stare, I went inside the hotel without giving him a chance to say any more.

My mask had been ripped off. I was furious with this maniac of a father who was destroying my life, and I didn’t know how to stop him. It was only a matter of time before the news reached all of my coworkers. They would find out that I had lied and pretended to be someone I was not. The management staff respected me, and I had built a good relationship with them. I had to get to them before someone else did, so I decided to talk to the personnel manager, Mr. Balasena.

He came to my office with some letters that he wanted typed. “I need to talk to you, sir. Can I come to your office?”

He looked at me with concern, nodded and walked back to his office. I followed him and stood in front of his desk. On the other side of his glass wall my coworkers were busy at their desks. Maybe they haven’t heard anything yet, I thought, and looked back at Mr. Balasena.

As I tried to gather my words, he said, “Trish, you’re a good worker, I like you a lot. Your personal life is none of my concern, so don’t worry about anything. I know you’re a good person and a wonderful worker. That’s all I need to know.”

My attempt had failed; it was too late to clear the air. Unsure how much he really knew, I thanked him and left his office.

Tears blocking my vision, I sat at my desk unable to make up my mind whether to quit my job or to take a leave of absence. I started to sense that the other workers had indeed heard something—there were small hints and whispers, questioning eyes and teasing laughter.

Finally I decided to take sick leave. As I reached the bus stop I saw Nuwan watching me, hidden inside a store. For a second I was tempted to let my guard down and run to him, to ask him how he was doing, if his parents had hurt him again, if they were following him around. But we couldn't risk being seen together; his father might be lurking in the vicinity. "I'm sorry Nuwan," I whispered to myself, walking away.

Nuwan's parents worried about their reputation, strove to live a spotless life and expected their children to be the best-behaved children in the world. Being the oldest child in the family, Nuwan had become the target for their harsh discipline, and when news of his involvement with an older woman reached them, it shattered their perfect world. It didn't matter to them what Nuwan had to say, or what he felt. All they wanted was to protect their image, and they were ready to go to any lengths to do so.

So they started their battle. Like a walking newspaper, they spread dirty rumors and even dropped in on my friends to trash me. The father visited Nuwan's workplace and asked his friends to watch him. "Nuwan is a dog in heat," he told them, "running after a rotten bitch who should be shot to death."

After two weeks at the convent, I went home. Nuwan's father guarded our house day and night, making sure his son didn't visit me. He was a shadow I couldn't get rid of, following me everywhere, watching me.

My parents, who had suffered a lifetime of shame, tried to protect us children from following in their footsteps. The pretense of wealth, along with all the restrictions and punishments, were meant to build a good reputation for us, but once I crossed the line and fell into the gutter, they didn't care about their image or any shame I might bring to the family. Even when Amma believed I had done wrong, she defended me to my relatives and neighbors and came to my rescue when necessary. My parents treated me like a human being. They advised me to stay away from Nuwan without demanding it. I realized what wonderful parents I had and felt terrible for Nuwan, having parents who didn't value his existence.

Once again my life was turned upside down. I didn't want to go back to work, or even out of my house; I couldn't ask my parents to move again, but then I couldn't bring more shame to them either. Once again, running away seemed to be my only option.

And so I quit the job I had loved so much, packed my bags, and with Samadha in tow flew to Pakistan to be with my sister Seetha. With Amma and Pappa's blessing Seetha had married an Adventist boy with whom she had fallen in love while in nursing school. Married for several years, she still lived with her in-laws in a two-story house; the parents, two sisters and a brother occupied the first floor, while Seetha and her husband and son had a bedroom and small living room upstairs. Samadha and I slept in her living room. Even without us visiting, the house was crowded and no one had any privacy.

Seetha never had any free time with her husband. When he came home from work he spent the entire evening downstairs with his family. Seetha's in-laws were nice people and we got along fine. Still, I wished for my sister's sake that she could have her own household. "Why do you have to live with all of them—can't you rent a house and move out?" I asked, after seeing what she was going through.

"I don't think we can ever move out. Gerald is the oldest in the family; he has to take care of his parents."

"So do you have to live with them forever? Why can't you move away and still take care of them?"

"They expect him to live with them, and Gerald is not going to hurt their feelings by moving out."

Every day after the family members went to work, I spent time with Seetha, hanging around her like a puppy as she did household chores and cooked special Pakistani dishes for me. She resisted my attempts to help her. I showed her the scars on my back. "I'm so sorry for what you went through, and for not being there to help you," she moaned. Like children we cried in each other's arms. In her presence I felt like a little girl again, but this time, rather than playing the jealous, spiteful younger sister, I loved her back.

Seetha helped me find a secretarial job and got Samadha admitted into a Christian English school. Things would have worked out if Seetha had had her own place or I had the chance to live on my own, but Seetha didn't like the idea of my living away from her. Like my parents, she was looking out for me, and I felt hemmed in.

Seetha's son Daniel was spoiled by his grandparents and started to make trouble for Samadha. Once Daniel bit Samadha's stomach and ran to his grandmother crying. She tried to comfort him and was hard on Samadha. I took my son aside and asked him what really had happened. He rolled up his shirt and bared the marks of teeth on his stomach.

Taking him in my arms, I held him close. How much more is he going to suffer for my mistakes? I asked myself. But blaming myself wasn't enough; I had to make new plans, and that night I decided to go back home. Father

Devin was right: It was time that I lived my life, doing what I thought was right and not caring what the world thought of me. We flew back home a couple of months after arriving, just in time to enroll Samadha in Maristella School for the third term.

After the prolonged absence I couldn't very well go back to the hotel job. Instead, I went to an employment agency and took on temporary assignments. That way, I thought, Nuwan's parents wouldn't be able to locate me. Like a bodyguard, my mother walked me to and from the bus stop.

Nuwan had moved out of his house and was living on his own, still determined to be a priest and to be independent of his parents. Their outrageous harassment had pushed him closer to me. No matter how hard I tried to distance myself from him, he wouldn't let me get away with it. Any chance he got, he called me or watched me from a distance. We started to see each other again, but now our meetings were handled with the utmost discretion. Not even my parents knew I was seeing him. Nuwan's father still had his relatives and friends watching us, so we had to go the extra mile to continue our friendship, meeting in different towns far away from home where no one would recognize us. Using my friend Nelum as a cover or taking time off from work, I met with Nuwan whenever possible.

"Let's go to Galle," Nuwan suggested one day. "I want to introduce you to my friend, Arjuna."

"A friend? Haven't they done enough harm to us? Why would this one be any different?"

"He's a Jesuit seminarian and my very best friend. He won't do anything to hurt me."

We talked about it for days before I agreed. We met under the Bo tree in Colombo, which had become our favorite rendezvous, and boarded the bus for Galle, a three-hour ride. Passing the city, suburbs and beaches along the way, we felt very relaxed and free of fear.

"Are we going to stay at the seminary?" I asked him.

"Are you crazy? They'd throw him out of there in a heartbeat! He's booked us in a hotel close to the seminary. He said it's a beautiful place right by the sea. I'm sure you'll like it."

That was the first time we were going to spend the night together in a hotel. It could be awkward, I thought, but it didn't scare me.

When we reached Galle it was late afternoon, and my back was hurting from sitting so long.

"It's a short walk but if you're too tired we can take a taxi," Nuwan said, sensing my discomfort.

"I'll be fine, let's walk," I said, annoyed with myself for not being stronger. We followed the directions Arjuna had given to the hotel. It was up on a hill, hidden behind a beautiful park; I liked the surroundings, the secrecy, the romantic atmosphere. I sat in the parlor while Nuwan checked us in, and when he came back with the keys we went up to the second floor. When we walked through the door the double bed stared at us, and I looked at him.

"They didn't have rooms with two beds available," he said.

"Fine," I said, looking away.

"I'll sleep on the floor if that makes you more comfortable," Nuwan said.

"It's okay, don't worry about it now." I trusted him.

Nuwan sat on the green bedspread and started to dial the phone on the nightstand at the side of the bed.

I went to the window and opened the striped sage curtains. The view took my breath away. There was a balcony overlooking the sea, with steps leading directly to the rocky coastline. I walked down them. The water was at its bluest and the waves were calm, gently caressing the rocks.

"How beautiful!" Nuwan said, right behind me. "Arjuna's on his way. Don't you want to rest a little while I wait for him?"

I went back into the room and lay down. Shortly there was a knock on the door. Within seconds, Nuwan jumped to the door and Arjuna came in. Sitting on the edge of the bed, I waited as they hugged each other. With excitement in his voice, Nuwan said, "This is Trish."

Arjuna turned around and saw me for the first time. His big eyes widened in disbelief. No telling what sort of picture he had in his mind, after all the rumors that had been flying around.

"Hello," he said with a smile.

"Hello, it's nice to finally see you in person," I said, smiling back. Though uncomfortable with the situation, I tried to be as nice I could, seeing how excited Nuwan was.

Arjuna took us to explore the natural harbor where the Europeans had first arrived in Sri Lanka. Three of us walked hand in hand on the beach and ran after each other like children, took pictures and lay in the sand and sang together. I sang Nuwan's favorite song, "*Sandakada Pahana*." I began to see how close Arjuna and Nuwan were. Like one soul in two bodies, they loved the same things and shared the same dreams. At sunset we sat quietly on the beach, enchanted by the sun dipping into the horizon in all its crimson and gold glory.

When finally we returned to the room it was dark and we ordered room service: fried rice, sweet and sour chicken and deviled fish.

I was my father's daughter—I could read thoughts—and despite the joyful afternoon we had spent together Arjuna's eyes betrayed the skepticism in his heart. But unlike Nuwan's parents, Arjuna was able to put doubt aside. He tried to be happy for Nuwan; I respected him for that.

The whole day had been a new experience for me, and I had relished every minute of it. After Arjuna left, Nuwan and I stayed out on the balcony listening to the ocean, closer than ever before. He made me feel as if it was safe to love him and to receive his love. The world had accused us of being lovers when we had just been friends. They had given us the key to the door that we had tried so hard not to open. Now, we didn't believe we had to control our feelings anymore—to satisfy the world by not sharing the love we felt for each other.

One touch, one kiss made us want more. I came alive in his arms; for the first time in my life, my heart experienced the joy of physical love. My skin ached for his touch and my body screamed with desire, blood rushed through my veins and my flesh melted in his arms as we consummated the love that had been suppressed for so long. We shared a love that was true in the eyes of God, a bond of heart, body and soul. In the act of love I forgot who I was. Later, looking at myself in the mirror, I saw a young face, not the face of a mother but the face of a girl, a bud that had been crushed and that had bloomed again. We spent the entire night in each other's arms, in a world of our own where no rules existed.

When we came back from Galle the next day and went our separate ways, everything was different. We were a couple now—lovers, as the world had assumed, but not in the way the world thought of lovers. Our souls had met, and we had become one. Happy—at last I was truly happy!

Still, neither of us had any desire to be married. "I don't need a certificate to love you—I'll always love you, even after death, nothing will ever change that," he vowed.

In Nuwan's mind, loving me didn't prevent him from serving God. "How could it be wrong to love someone the way I love you and to serve God at the same time?" Despite his love for me, Nuwan still wanted desperately to become a priest.

While he confronted this issue, I struggled with guilt. Nuwan was only twenty-four and I was thirty. I convinced myself that I would let him be free whenever he wanted out, but I wouldn't be the one to break it off. I could never destroy him by walking away.

My past continued to shadow me. Nuwan's parents found out—how, I don't know—that we were still seeing each other, and in an effort to dig up dirt they had gone to Chilaw, my mother's hometown, and gathered rumors about my past. One day, equipped with that information, they dropped in on Amma while Pappa was off at work. Nuwan's father started yelling at my mother, blaming her for our relationship, and the neighbors came spilling out of their houses.

"This is a whore family, the mother and daughter drugged my child and seduced him," he shouted. Addressing the neighbors, he said, "Do you know what kind of a family lives in your neighborhood? The mother is the biggest tramp; this is her second husband, that man who calls himself a doctor and has had three wives! He was also a priest before he got married, now, what kind of man could do that? Be a priest and then get married, not just once but three times? Those are the examples they set for their children. Their daughter went to Lebanon to be a prostitute and she was caught in the act with a man, and his wife pushed this whore over the balcony! They broke her back, but still no one can stop her from seducing men!"

Amma, who had gone out on the porch, was publicly humiliated; I stayed inside the house cowering, glad Pappa wasn't home because if he had been it would have turned into a nasty fight.

"If you need a real man come to me, I can give you a stomach full, if that's not enough I'll send you every man in my town," he screamed.

Amma came back inside, trembling. "Please make him stop," I whispered.

She held me in her arms. "Why in the world did you get involved with Nuwan? If you want to get married I can find you a good man; you don't have to listen to this kind of accusation. This man is a low-brow, ignorant fool who has no shame. He won't let you have a peaceful life if you don't stop this friendship."

It was deeply disturbing to me that Nuwan's parents were attacking my parents again, and I was upset with myself for ruining their reputation. Still, marriage was not an option; my commitment to single motherhood hadn't changed just because I was in love. How could I explain this to my mother? If only Father Devin were around, I thought, but he was thousands of miles away on a mission trip.

The neighbors believed all the scandalous talk; they laughed at me and talked behind my back. It wasn't pleasant, but this time I didn't hide. I held my head up high, ignoring their whispers, and walked passed them. If people stared at me, I would stop and stare them down until they looked away.

My mother went to the police and made a complaint against Nuwan's parents. When Amma was called before the police inspector for a hearing, the claim was turned against her; the inspector warned her to keep Nuwan away from our house and not to let me carry on our relationship. Amma was sure that Nuwan's father had bribed the police officer.

I decided not to put up with it any longer; I told Nuwan that if he wanted to be in my life, he had to put a stop to his parents' harassment. If he didn't, he could never see me again. He promised to stay away until he found a way to control his parents.

A couple of days later he called me at work and asked me to meet him under the Bo tree at the Pettah bus stand. Not wanting to argue on the phone, I agreed. From the Bo tree we took a taxi to a nearby park. It was the only safe place we had to spend a couple of hours together. We sat near a pond hidden behind the huge trees, and he took my hands in his. His eyes were bright, his smile teasing. "My parents won't bother you again."

"Just like that?" I said doubtfully, not believing he had the courage to stand up to them. "How can you be sure? They'll find a way to kill me."

He kissed my hands. "I played my last trump card on them. Do you remember the police inspector who took my father's side? Well, he's a very good friend of my father, and I paid him a visit. I had a long talk with him and told him how my parents had treated me all these years. I also made a police entry against my parents—if they try to harass you or your parents in any way again, I threatened that I would marry you on that day."

"Why do you think it will stop your parents?"

"Don't you see? This is what they were trying to avoid by harassing you. Now my threat to marry you will control them from coming after you. If they don't take me seriously and they continue their harassment, we'll get married. Then you'll be my wife, and there's nothing anyone can do about it."

"But I'm not going to marry you. I can't do that to you—you want to be a priest."

He pulled me close to him, looking around to make sure no one was watching, then gently kissed me.

"If worse comes to worse, we'll get married. It will be only a signature on paper; we don't have to act like husband and wife. We can live the way we live now, you with your parents, and me by myself. After a few years, once my parents have forgotten that we exist, we get a divorce. You're not planning to marry anyone any time soon, and I can wait all my life to be a priest," he said, with a big grin.

"Oh yes, they'll let you be a priest after being married and divorced!" I said sarcastically.

"Things will change by then. Why can't I serve the Lord just because I had a woman in my life? Cheating and adultery are wrong, but I will have only one partner for my whole life, and how can that be wrong? Even Jesus had a woman friend. I think He loved Mary just the way I love you."

His reasoning was odd, to be sure, but I was relieved and hoped that his threat would work. He agreed to stay away from my house and to take precautions to avoid any outburst from his parents.

A few months went by without a sound from his parents, and it seemed as if the threat had worked. They didn't come to my parents again, although they sent threatening letters to me. "*You'd better be careful of unfortunate accidents*," one read. Without mentioning them to Amma and Pappa I threw the missives away, wondering if Nuwan's parents would ever make good on their threat.

Chapter 15

It was by chance that I visited the Baptist church one Sunday morning. Alex, a patient of Pappa's, had invited me to attend his church service, and after it ended he introduced me to a group of Canadians and Americans who resided in Sri Lanka. They were evangelists who worked for a company in Katunayake, the free-trade zone where foreigners had their businesses. The zone was under strict security and no one was able to enter it without a pass. One of the people I met that morning at church, Mr. Falkner, asked me if I knew any Sri Lankan woman who might apply for a position as a personal secretary in his company, Christian Literature, a printing press that published Bibles and Christian literature. He said they had computers. Excited, I told him I would love to apply for the position.

It was 1985 and computer technology was new to Sri Lanka. It would be the chance of a lifetime to become computer literate, and the free-trade zone would be a safe haven where Nuwan's parents' tentacles couldn't reach me. So I applied for the job, and was surprised to see Mr. Falkner seated at the managing director's desk. He greeted me with a friendly smile and bent over—he was twice as tall—to shake my hand. Happy with my resume and experience, he hired me as his personal secretary.

It was a dream job. The management staff were Baptists from Sweden, Norway, Canada and the United States. My desk was on the first floor next to the director's office. Matthew Reed, a Canadian who was the computer brain, shared the whole first floor with me. Four women worked as data-entry operators on the ground floor. The printing press, a few yards away from the main building, had twenty employees. They translated the Bible into other languages, and I learned the art of creating Sinhala characters on the computer using the English keyboard.

Matthew took a keen interest in teaching me and we became good friends. Once I got used to the basic functions of the computer, I borrowed manuals from Matthew and learned all the word-processing packages available at the time. He taught me how to use the database Lotus and various other software packages.

Mr. Olausson, the chairman of the company, was a Christian who had spent all of his life as a missionary. He suffered from spinal cancer and had to go to Norway for treatment every six months. He had no children, and I heard that his wife was many years older than he. Observing their love for each other, I tried to convince myself that it was not wrong to be involved with Nuwan. No one at the press looked down on me for being a single mother; I didn't have to lie to them about my past or pretend to be someone I was not. They treated me with respect and saw me as a hard-working woman. They were wonderful, honest and caring people.

The informal workplace and the friendly management staff made for a good team. The people who worked at Christian Literature were like family to me. They visited my home, and sometimes I took them around the neighborhood. When Matthew dropped by, I didn't think anything of it, but Amma grew curious. She sensed that he was interested in me. "He's a Canadian, Amma. Why would he be interested in a Sri Lankan?" was my response. Then one day Matthew asked me to take a ride with him in his new car. I liked annoying the neighbors by associating with foreigners. Once I heard someone say, "Now she's found a foreigner!"

"Oh, no," her companion said. "Not just one—she has many men, young and old."

On Secretary's Day, Matthew took me to lunch at the Hilton Hotel in the heart of Colombo. After lunch we sat outside on the balcony facing the sea. The Sri Lankan stewards were watching me curiously, trying to figure out what I was doing in a hotel with a foreigner. I ignored their glances and tried to have fun on my day off from work. We talked about a lot of things. Matthew asked me about my family and why I was still single.

"I never had a girlfriend, and I find myself thinking about you all the time," he said out of the blue. "I like you a lot, Trish."

Caught off guard, I pretended not to understand what he meant. "I like you too, Matthew," was all I could think to say.

He looked at me with his pale blue eyes. "I'd like to be more than a friend to you. We can take it slow. We can go to Canada and live a wonderful life."

"Why me?" I stammered, trying to hide my shock. "You know I was married before and I have a child. Doesn't that bother you?"

"Why should it matter if you were married before? You're a free woman now. I can promise to be a good father to your son."

There were two little problems—I was not interested in marriage, and I was in love with Nuwan.

Nonetheless, the fact that this man was willing to marry me, that my past didn't stigmatize me in his eyes, lifted my spirit. It was as if a whole new world of possibility was opening up before me, a world where I could be both loved and respected.

My heart was tempted. This could be the chance of a lifetime, I thought, a chance to leave my troubles behind and start a new life.

"You don't have to give me an answer right now," Matthew went on. "Take all the time you need. My parents aren't too keen about mixed marriages but I'll talk to them."

Like Nuwan, Matthew had never been married before and he was six years younger than I. It didn't seem to matter to the foreigners. In their eyes I was just another woman who was available. If only I could leave this country, I kept thinking, I could find freedom, acceptance, a life without shame!

Had it not been for Nuwan, I would have taken Matthew's offer. Instead, I began thinking that maybe Nuwan and I could be happy in a different country, in a place where we would be accepted as a couple, freed from the chains of the past. We could be happy and free! A tiny seed of hope grew in me. All we wanted now was the freedom to love each other, nothing more.

A couple of days later I saw Nuwan and told him about Matthew's proposal. "If you want to marry him, if you think he can make you happy, that's all right with me, I won't stand in your way. I'll always love you."

How could a man love a woman the way he loved me and accept her marriage to someone else? Those words made me love him even more, for loving me so unselfishly.

There was no need to keep Matthew waiting. When I saw him at work the next day, I told him that we should just remain friends. Though he was disappointed, he agreed and I continued to enjoy his company and support at work.

Meanwhile, I began to think of a way to leave Sri Lanka in search of freedom.

Months later I was invited to lunch with Mr. Olausson's family. They lived in a huge house close to my home, which they shared with other foreign workers. We all sat at the table and I pretended to enjoy their pasta and salad. After clearing the table, I went into the kitchen to see if they needed any help. Mr. Olausson was at the sink washing dishes. I was not used to seeing a man working in the kitchen and offered to help him.

"Mrs. Olausson is going to kill me if I don't do my share of the work," he laughed.

"Let him do his share," Mrs. Olausson said as she came out of her bedroom. She took my hand and we walked out into the yard and sat under a tall mango tree surrounded by rose bushes.

Mrs. Olausson, a big woman, twice my size, was in her seventies, but she had the courage of a twenty-year-old.

"Mr. Olausson was dying in the hospital when he had a vision from God. He was asked to come to Sri Lanka to spread the Lord's word," she said. "He had no idea where Sri Lanka was but he decided to come here, and when he did he got better."

Presently Mr. Olausson came and joined us. "So what are your future plans, Trish?" he asked.

"I don't know, sir," I said, puzzled by his question. "Life here isn't easy for me. I'd like to emigrate to Europe and enjoy the freedom."

"Could you please not call me sir? Call me Erling."

"Yes, sir," I said, and they laughed. In Sri Lanka it was disrespectful to call your elders by their first names, and I couldn't bring myself to do otherwise.

"I'm one person who is strictly against mixed marriages," Mr. Olausson said. "I've seen the struggle couples go through trying to deal with two cultures. But you, Trish, I would have approved of your marriage to Matthew. You're a wonderful woman who would have adjusted well to Canada."

"It means a lot to me that you think I'm a good person. In Sri Lanka, I've been condemned forever for my past mistakes."

"I don't understand this culture," Mrs. Olausson said. "The people are so nice and kind to us, they have good family values, but in some ways they're narrow-minded and stubborn."

I told them that I had been toying with the idea of leaving Sri Lanka, that I wanted to find a way to be independent and didn't want to live with my parents forever. It was my turn to take care of them.

"Don't leave Sri Lanka, Trish," said Mr. Olausson. "You'd forget who you are and lose all your values. If I can help you to start your own business, would you consider staying here?"

I was stunned, and thought he was joking.

"I know you like computers," he went on. "If I sponsor you, can you manage a small computer institute? Everything is so expensive in Sri Lanka. I'd like you to open a computer school and charge less than the other schools. That way you'd be helping poor children who want to learn computers, and you'd also attract more students."

"Are you serious about this, sir?" I asked doubtfully. Mrs. Olausson winked at me and smiled cheerfully.

"I want to help you, Trish. If you decide you want to do this, let me know. I'll give you the computers and take care of the start-up costs."

Why does he think I can do this? I wondered. What is it he sees in me that I don't? It sounded like an impossible dream, but if I could do it, it would be my ticket to freedom. I could be a respected figure in society. If I had money people would forget my past...

"I'll think about it, sir. Thank you for trusting me and believing in me."

As I said goodbye, Mrs. Olausson gave me a big bosomy hug. "You can do it, child, God will help you," she said.

Though I craved the opportunity, I went home doubting I could handle the responsibility. I talked to my parents and they encouraged me to go ahead with the idea. But it was Nuwan who gave me the confidence that I needed.

Excited about the opportunity, he envisioned how it could be done and promised to help with the setup, assuring me that meanwhile he would keep his parents from harming me.

Having been with a computer company for many years, Nuwan had made good contacts in the computer field and introduced me to some of them. They too supported the idea and agreed to help in any way they could. After a few weeks of research with Nuwan, I was convinced that Mr. Olausson's idea could become a reality.

Sitting at the reception desk, making sure everything was in place, I laughed with delight. Was this for real? The sunlight seeped through the passion vine onto the porch. The first bloom had appeared on the vine. A spatter of rain had roiled up the dust in the streets. I went out into the cleanly swept yard and a mango leaf waltzed in the breeze and landed on my hair. Two poles rooted in the ground held the sign proudly in place. The bold black lettering danced in front of my eyes: Futuresoft Computer Services.

It was the opening day of school, in a huge rented house in Kandana, about ten miles from Colombo. The living room and one bedroom had been converted into a lecture hall and a computer room; the open front porch and another room were the reception area. The rest of the house was reserved for my use: two bedrooms, two bathrooms, a large dining room and a good-sized kitchen. I was one of the few people who had a telephone in town.

Excited but nervous, I awaited the arrival of my parents and a few good friends to celebrate the occasion. First to arrive was Nuwan, along with some friends of his who had enrolled as students. Then Pappa and Amma showed up. My mother helped me set the table. We covered it with a white tablecloth and spread out the *kiribath,* milk rice, and some sweets she had prepared.

Surrounded by friends and family, I lit one of seven oil wicks on a lamp, a gesture symbolizing a new beginning. Mr. Olausson delivered the opening remarks, focusing on how the school would benefit the public. Mr. Weerasinghe, one of the professors I had hired to teach computer programming, gave an introduction to computers, driving home the point that they "think" only by responding to external commands. From the expressions on their faces, it was clear that the students liked their professor. While all this was going on, Pappa and Amma sat proudly in the last row of the lecture hall. Amma still worried for my safety, but finally I had made her happy.

That night was my first alone in the house with Samadha. I walked from one room to another, searching every corner, closing all the windows and locking the doors. After placing plastic covers over the computers to protect them from dust, I switched off the lights and sat in the lecture hall. The white rectangular board glowed in the dark. Instead of going to bed, I knelt down to pray and cried, thanking the Lord for all that He had given me.

Samadha was fast asleep in my bed. The noises outside kept me alert, and I was on edge being alone. That was a small price to pay for finally reaching my goals. Life couldn't get any better than this—I was free and living on my own, managing my own school. In addition, Mr. Olausson had authorized me to sell the Sinhala word-processing package created by Matthew. It was a lot of work but the challenge was thrilling.

Nuwan lived only a few miles from my home. With his support I was able to hire the best professors and get good prices for advertising services. We still had to keep our distance in public and pretended to be strangers to each other. There was little time for us to get away and hide from prying eyes. I had built a new life, but still I was hiding from my past.

Matthew came by often to help me with the accounts. Mr. Olausson and his wife visited the school regularly, as did my parents. Among other visitors was the secretary for my old Adventist mission. I was surprised when he dropped and asked me to join the staff at the boarding school in Kandy.

"Why do you think I would close down my school to come teach in yours?" I said.

"Computers are new in our school and we don't have any good teachers. We can pay you more than you make now."

It was my turn to speak the truth. "Where were you when I needed support? Where were you when they crossed my name off the membership? Where were you when I tried to get my son into your school?" I paused and thought, why am I attacking this poor man? He'd had nothing to do with how the mission discriminated against me. "I'm sorry," I said, "but I can't help you. I'm happy right here."

"I'm sorry for the way we treated you. Can't you forgive us and come back to us as a Christian?" he said.

"But I'm not a Christian in your eyes, and not a member of your mission. I do believe in God and serve Him the way I feel is right. I would rather help the people who were there for me when I was down. In my eyes they are the real Christians," I said, thinking of Mr. Olausson.

God had spared my life and made it better, but I had to pay the consequences for my actions. Jumping off the balcony was my choice, and the never-ending pain in my back was the payback for the path I had taken. I was never going to recover completely. Walking normally and looking normal was just a cover-up; inside I always hurt. Cooking, cleaning, even washing dishes was too much for me, and though I tried to keep house, when my back started aching I had to lie down and rest. The pain had become a part of me. But instead of destroying my spirit, it gave me courage.

Doreen, a teenager who had once been my mother's helper, came to work for me, and Amma continued to be a saint, tending to me without being asked, rubbing the herbal ointment into my back and doing various household chores.

One day Samadha and I were walking home from town. The sun was setting and a merciless wind swept the streets, covering us with dust. Samadha walked a few yards ahead of me, carrying a bag of guava, his favorite fruit. I had just picked up some fresh *malupann* (fish buns) from the bakery and was helping myself to one when suddenly I heard a man cursing from a passing motorbike. Heart pounding, I glanced back and saw Nuwan's parents staring back at me. The motorbike skidded to a stop, turned around and came barreling toward me. Grabbing Samadha's hand,

I broke into a run, desperately casting my eyes about for a place to hide, and spotted a side street. We dashed up a tiny pathway that led to a house and, without a clue what I would say to the owners, hid behind the concrete wall surrounding the house. Luckily the owners didn't appear.

"Why are we hiding, Ammy?" Samadha asked.

"Be quiet," I whispered, wondering what to tell him. About a half an hour later we came out of hiding, looked cautiously around and walked home.

"Why did we hide, Ammy?" Samadha pressed.

"Don't worry about it, Putha. I thought someone was coming after us, but I was wrong." I managed a weak smile. Doubtfully, he studied my face, then let go of my hand and ran inside the house.

After that I limited my outdoor activities, never going anywhere alone.

The nights grew worse. Surrounded by a fenced-in yard, with all the doors and windows locked, with Bunty, my little white dog, under the bed and Mino, a German shepherd, guarding the door, I would lie in bed paralyzed with fear, thinking Nuwan's parents might send someone after me. Whenever Mino barked and scampered toward the door, I would start sweating. Every noise startled me. Footsteps outside kept me up all night, and finally at dawn I would fall asleep, promising myself to be stronger the following night.

The ongoing war between the Tamils and Sinhalese didn't make life any easier. Violence was rampant, and people took advantage of the general chaos to rob their enemies and destroy their property. To make matters worse, the People's Liberation Front, brutally crushed back in 1970, resurfaced in 1989. The government closed down schools and businesses, a curfew was declared and once again all of Sri Lanka turned into a battlefield. Though Nuwan kept a close eye on me, I was afraid his parents would seize their advantage and hire someone to murder me. Whenever possible Amma came to spend the night; that was the only time I ever got any sleep.

One afternoon Nuwan rushed into my house and called me to the office where we usually discussed our problems without being disturbed. "If you had a chance to go to America, would you leave all this behind and come with me?"

"You mean the United States of America?"

"Yes!"

"Are you teasing me? How can we go to America?"

"Well, we can migrate to States, do you want to try this? Think of the life we could have together! I could be with you all the time; we wouldn't have to answer to anyone. We might even find a cure for your pain!"

He sounded excited and convincing. His eyes were filled with love, and there was a smile on his face as he held mine between his palms.

"Let me take care of you. Lean on me, I'll never let you fall."

By this time Nuwan had given up his dream of becoming a priest. In my eyes, however, he was as holy now as he'd ever been. He was still the same Good Samaritan, just without the collar. The amazing thing was that he had managed to break away from his parents and find happiness in his love for me. Now all we wanted was the liberty to love each other. America would be our passport to freedom.

"Yes," I said, envisioning us walking hand in hand down the busy streets of America, "if I could go there I would leave all this behind."

But I doubted our chances. The United States was the richest country in the world, the land of opportunity. Only the best of the best went there. Going to America seemed like a fairy tale.

After surviving so many hurdles, Samadha and I had almost everything we needed in life—a better place in society, good friends, money and independence. What we lacked was security. This, I thought, might be my chance to protect Samadha from the horrors of war, to offer him a peaceful life. It also would also mean a life with Nuwan, an opportunity for us to love each other to the fullest, even to get married. How wonderful life would be if we had the freedom to love without fear.

We spent the next few months trying to make our dream a reality. With the help of his friend, Nuwan made all the necessary arrangements for us to migrate to the United States. I could hardly believe our luck.

I met with Mr. Olausson and promised to sell everything and pay him back the money I owed him. He was understanding. The computer school had been closed for many months anyway, due to the on-and-off curfew, and there was no certainty as to when I might be back in business. After informing the students of my decision and referring them to a friend of mine who taught computer courses, I shut down the school and sold the computers and all the materials.

Samadha, thirteen years old now, was excited about going to America. Only a few days remained before our departure, and I thought it would be a good excuse to get him together with his father one more time. It was my last chance to free his heart from the hate he felt for Tilak. We were enjoying our last few days with Pappa and Amma, at their house. "Don't you want to say goodbye to your father?" I asked him.

"I don't know… I don't think he wants to see me."

"It doesn't matter what he wants, I'd like you to say goodbye to your father before you leave. This is your chance to say what you feel about him. Just do your part and set yourself free. Don't worry about him."

He sat quietly for a few minutes, then said skeptically, "If you think I should see him before I leave, I'll do it, Ammy."

I made the arrangements with Nuwan, who contacted Tilak and requested a meeting in Marawila so Tilak's family wouldn't have to be involved. Tilak agreed, and on the day of the meeting Nuwan left them alone for a couple of hours while he watched from a distance.

When Samadha came back home that day, he looked different. When I questioned him about the meeting he said, "Nothing for you to worry about, Ammy; it's between my father and me." He never breathed a word to me about the content of their conversation; whatever it was, he no longer hated his father or longed for him. From that day on, Samadha acted more like a grownup. Finally, I could lead him to a better life, with no strings attached.

Although she was afraid that Nuwan's parents would try to hurt me, Amma wasn't happy about us leaving. "I'm sorry to see you breaking up the nest you've built for yourself and your son."

"I'll build a better one, Amma. I'm not alone this time."

"I know, that's the only comfort I have, knowing Nuwan is there to help you and you'll be safe from his parents."

Sitting beside my father, I rested my head on his shoulder and pulled the springy gray curls on his neck.

"When the ship starts to sink, all the mice run away," he said, smiling.

"I'm not abandoning you, Pappa! This is a chance I have to take, it doesn't matter where or how far away I live, I'll always love you and support you financially."

"I know, but your brothers and sisters are all over the world," he said. "You're the only one who stayed close to me. I'm going to miss you badly."

Somehow he knew this time I was leaving for good, and with deep-seated sadness I kissed his cheeks, rested my head on his chest and felt his fingers caressing my hair, the only way we knew how to say we loved each other. It was the last time I would ever see him.

And so in search of freedom, I said goodbye to my family, my friends and my country. A new life lay ahead, with strangers in a strange land, but with no cloud of past transgressions hanging over my head. I had defied fate, refusing to accept a life of danger and condemnation, welcoming the unknown with the confidence of one who has already been put to the test. With Nuwan and Samadha by my side, I stepped onto the plane and into the future.

To Love is to Believe

Those who believe, risk death;
Endless Life flows thru' them.
May we so love as to believe!

Praise for In Contempt of Fate:

"In Contempt of Fate was an amazing read. I still don't know how this remarkable woman was able to survive".

Wendy Baumgartner, President of
American Book Readers Association.

"The author expertly uses descriptive details that draws the reader into her story. What will happen to Ranga, who yearns only to give her son a better life? Her plight as an indentured maid in a foreign land, stripped of the most basic rights, forbidden to contact her family is a poignant reminder of the thousands of women whose untold stories echo in darkness. A must read!"

Virginia Holmstrom,ExecutiveDirector,
American Baptist Churches.

"A story so poignant and compelling it touched my heart in many, many ways."

Reeve Lindbergh, author of "Under A
Wing", a memoir.